D0908944

Understanding World History

Elizabethan England

Other titles in the series include:

Ancient Egypt
Ancient Greece
Ancient Rome
Pearl Harbor
The Black Death
The Decade of the 2000s
The Digital Age
The Holocaust
The Early Middle Ages
The Late Middle Ages
The Renaissance

Understanding
World History

Elizabethan
England

Stuart A. Kallen

Bruno Leone
Series Consultant

ReferencePoint
Press®

San Diego, CA

© 2013 ReferencePoint Press, Inc.
Printed in the United States

For more information, contact:
ReferencePoint Press, Inc.
PO Box 27779
San Diego, CA 92198
www.ReferencePointPress.com

LIBRARY OF CONGRESS CATALOGING-IN-PUBLICATION DATA

Kallen, Stuart A., 1955-
  Elizabethan England / by Stuart A. Kallen.
    p. cm. -- (Understanding world history series)
  Includes bibliographical references and index.
  ISBN-13: 978-1-60152-484-3 (hardback)
  ISBN-10: 1-60152-484-6 (hardback)
  1. Great Britain--History--Elizabeth, 1558-1603. 2. England--Social conditions--16th century.
  3. England--Civilization--16th century. I. Title.
  DA355.K35 2012
  942.05'5--dc23
                                                                    2012026174

Contents

Foreword

When the Puritans first emigrated from England to America in 1630, they believed that their journey was blessed by a covenant between themselves and God. By the terms of that covenant they agreed to establish a community in the New World dedicated to what they believed was the true Christian faith. God, in turn, would reward their fidelity by making certain that they and their descendants would always experience his protection and enjoy material prosperity. Moreover, the Lord guaranteed that their land would be seen as a shining beacon—or in their words, a "city upon a hill,"—which the rest of the world would view with admiration and respect. By embracing this notion that God could and would shower his favor and special blessings upon them, the Puritans were adopting the providential philosophy of history—meaning that history is the unfolding of a plan established or guided by a higher intelligence.

The concept of intercession by a divine power is only one of many explanations of the driving forces of world history. Historians and philosophers alike have subscribed to numerous other ideas. For example, the ancient Greeks and Romans argued that history is cyclical. Nations and civilizations, according to these ancients of the Western world, rise and fall in unpredictable cycles; the only certainty is that these cycles will persist throughout an endless future. The German historian Oswald Spengler (1880–1936) echoed the ancients to some degree in his controversial study *The Decline of the West*. Spengler asserted that all civilizations inevitably pass through stages comparable to the life span of a person: childhood, youth, adulthood, old age, and, eventually, death. As the title of his work implies, Western civilization is currently entering its final stage.

Joining those who see purpose and direction in history are thinkers who completely reject the idea of meaning or certainty. Rather, they reason that since there are far too many random and unseen factors at work on the earth, historians would be unwise to endorse historical predictability of any type. Warfare (both nuclear and conventional), plagues, earthquakes, tsunamis, meteor showers, and other catastrophic world-changing events have loomed large throughout history and prehistory. In his essay "A Free Man's Worship," philosopher and mathematician Bertrand Russell (1872–1970) supported this argument, which many refer to as the nihilist or chaos theory of history. According to Russell, history follows no preordained path. Rather, the earth itself and all life on earth resulted from, as Russell describes it, an "accidental collocation of atoms." Based on this premise, he pessimistically concluded that all human achievement will eventually be "buried beneath the debris of a universe in ruins."

Whether history does or does not have an underlying purpose, historians, journalists, and countless others have nonetheless left behind a record of human activity tracing back nearly 6,000 years. From the dawn of the great ancient Near Eastern civilizations of Mesopotamia and Egypt to the modern economic and military behemoths China and the United States, humanity's deeds and misdeeds have been and continue to be monitored and recorded. The distinguished British scholar Arnold Toynbee (1889–1975), in his widely acclaimed twelve-volume work entitled *A Study of History,* studied twenty-one different civilizations that have passed through history's pages. He noted with certainty that others would follow.

In the final analysis, the academic and journalistic worlds mostly regard history as a record and explanation of past events. From a more practical perspective, history represents a sequence of building blocks—cultural, technological, military, and political—ready to be utilized and enhanced or maligned and perverted by the present. What that means is that all societies—whether advanced civilizations or preliterate tribal cultures—leave a legacy for succeeding generations to either embrace or disregard.

Recognizing the richness and fullness of history, the ReferencePoint Press Understanding World History series fosters an evaluation and interpretation of history and its influence on later generations. Each volume in the series approaches its subject chronologically and topically, with specific focus on nations, periods, or pivotal events. Primary and secondary source quotations are included, along with complete source notes and suggestions for further research.

Moreover, the series reflects the truism that the key to understanding the present frequently lies in the past. With that in mind, each series title concludes with a legacy chapter that highlights the bonds between past and present and, more important, demonstrates that world history is a continuum of peoples and ideas, sometimes hidden but there nonetheless, waiting to be discovered by those who choose to look.

Important Events in Elizabethan England

1509
Henry VIII becomes king of England and is soon married to Spanish princess Catherine of Aragon.

1475
William Caxton imports England's first printing press and begins publishing books in London.

1559
Parliament passes a new Act of Supremacy and the Act of Uniformity, establishing Protestantism as England's official religion.

1465　**1495**　**1525**　**1555**

1485
The first Tudor king, Henry VII, ascends the throne.

1534
Parliament passes the Act of Supremacy, which ends all papal authority in England (and is later repealed by Mary I).

1553
Mary becomes queen and reestablishes Catholicism as the official religion.

1558
Mary dies; Elizabeth I becomes queen of England, and the Elizabethan era begins.

1568
John Hawkins's fleet of pirate ships is destroyed by Spanish warships near Veracruz, Mexico, setting off a decades-long conflict between England and Spain.

1574
In a privateering mission sanctioned by Elizabeth, Francis Drake robs a mule train outside Nombre de Dios, Panama, and steals a fortune in gold and silver.

1563
Parliament passes the first of a series of acts called the Poor Laws to provide relief to those living in poverty.

1599
The Globe Theater opens in London with a performance of Shakespeare's *Julius Caesar*.

1560   **1570**   **1580**   **1590**   **1600**

1576
James Burbage builds the first freestanding playhouse, an amphitheater called The Theatre, in Shoreditch outside London.

1601
Parliament passes the Poor Relief Act, creating a system of workhouses that remained operative until the late nineteenth century.

1564
On April 23 playwright William Shakespeare is born in Stratford-upon-Avon.

1588
The English Royal Navy defeats the Spanish Armada near Calais, France.

1603
On March 24 Elizabeth dies at age sixty-nine; King James I ascends the throne.

The Defining Characteristics of Elizabethan England

The Elizabethan era began on November 17, 1558, when Elizabeth Tudor was crowned queen of England. Around that time, a royal clerk named Armigal Waad compiled a catalog of woes challenging England: "The Queen poor. The realm exhausted. The nobility poor and decayed. Want of good captains and soldiers. The people out of order. Justice not executed. All things dear [expensive]."[1]

Waad was correct. When Elizabeth I ascended the throne, England was on the brink of ruin. In the previous decades the nation had been torn asunder by religious conflicts between Catholics and Protestants. The royal treasury had been drained by Elizabeth's predecessors, who had engaged in a series of futile and expensive wars. Foreign trade was at an all-time low, causing financial problems for the fifty to sixty families that made up England's aristocracy. The lives of Elizabeth's other 4.5 million subjects were, for the most part, governed by poverty, ignorance, starvation, and disease.

A Nation Transformed

Few subjects of the realm believed the new queen, who was only twenty-five years old, could solve their problems. Yet almost immediately, Elizabeth set England on a course that vastly improved the nation's fortunes. For the following forty-four years of Elizabeth's reign, a time known as the Elizabethan era, England was transformed from a poor, backward nation into a world power.

At Elizabeth's behest, Parliament made Protestantism the official religion of England. This helped put an end to decades of conflict between Catholics and Protestants over religious matters. In later years the queen balanced England's budget with gold and jewels plundered by royal privateers (like John Hawkins and Francis Drake) who were licensed by the crown to attack enemy ships. Elizabethan explorers Martin Frobisher and Walter Raleigh expanded Elizabeth's realm, planting the English flag in New World colonies in North America.

While her pirates roved the high seas, Elizabeth avoided war at home and encouraged foreign trade. This spurred an economic boom that helped to enrich the earls, lords, ladies, viscounts, barons, dukes, duchesses, and knights who made up the nation's nobility. The growing wealth also helped create a new middle class, people who worked as merchants, professors, gardeners, lawyers, and artisans.

Economic expansion during the Elizabethan era fueled the English Renaissance in art, literature, and science. Unlike Italy, England did not produce great Renaissance painters like Michelangelo, Leonardo da Vinci, and Sandro Botticelli. The English Renaissance took place mainly in London playhouses, which were among the most crowded in Europe. Attending plays was seen as the height of fashion and sophistication. By the end of the 1600s, rich and poor alike regularly attended plays by William Shakespeare, Ben Jonson, Christopher Marlowe, and other celebrated playwrights.

The High and Mighty Empress

Elizabeth was among the skilled writers of the day. She authored her own speeches, poems, public prayers, government documents, and letters. Keenly aware of the power of words, the queen commissioned writers like Raleigh, Jonson, and Edmund Spenser to praise her in poems and stories. Spenser, who wrote the three-volume epic *The Faerie*

England's Queen Elizabeth I, in procession with her courtiers, looks every bit the glorious monarch who reigned for more than forty years. Though many of her subjects lived in poverty and filth, under Elizabeth the nation flourished in commerce, trade, science, and the arts.

Queene, dedicated the work to Elizabeth. He praised her in sixteenth-century language as "the most High, Mightie and Magnificent Empress renowned for pietie [piety], vertue [virtue] and all gratious [gracious] government."[2] Through such uses of artistic propaganda, the queen earned the nickname "Gloriana," which characterize her as an eternally youthful woman who symbolized England's strength and national unity.

Elizabeth remained unmarried her entire life and was often referred to by her subjects as the Virgin Queen. She had many suitors, including King Philip II of Spain and Archduke Charles of Austria. However, Elizabeth turned down their marriage proposals, stating that she was married to her kingdom and her people. This was seen as an example to her supporters, an inducement to spend their lives and wealth in the service of their country.

Sewage, Fires, and Plagues

The Elizabethan era ended when Queen Elizabeth died on March 24, 1603. In the aftermath of her death, she continued to be honored by historians, artists, and writers. By the 1800s Elizabeth was widely viewed as a wise, intelligent, and beloved ruler. In the nineteenth century the Elizabethan era was often referred to as England's golden age. However, the glories of Elizabeth's reign provided few benefits to the 95 percent of English citizens who were not privileged. In the countryside nearly everyone labored from sunup to sundown, lived in hovels, and rarely had enough food to eat. Within crowded London the poor resided in filthy slums, where raw sewage ran through the streets, fires regularly incinerated entire neighborhoods, and periodic plague epidemics killed thousands.

Despite the poor conditions in which many of her subjects lived, Elizabeth undeniably ruled a nation that was rapidly advancing in commerce, trade, science, and the arts. The queen financed the expansion of the Royal Navy, which allowed England to triumph over its powerful enemy, Spain. With foresight and determination to improve the lot of her people, Elizabeth laid the foundation for modern Britain. By 1700 England was the most powerful nation on earth.

Chapter 1

What Conditions Led to the Elizabethan Era?

The Elizabethan era, which lasted from 1558 to 1603, is remembered as a time of dramatic changes in England. Daring English sea captains explored Asia, Africa, and the Americas; the London theater ignited a literary Renaissance; and Protestantism replaced Catholicism as the nation's dominant religion. All of these endeavors were built upon revolutionary changes that occurred years before the reign of Queen Elizabeth I.

The major events that led to the Elizabethan Era took place primarily on the European continent. They include the invention of the printing press, improvements in ship construction, and the Protestant Reformation.

A Desire for Knowledge

The Elizabethan era began a little more than a century after the invention of the printing press. Before the technique of printing with movable type was perfected by Johannes Gutenberg in Mainz, Germany, around 1450, books were rare and expensive. One book could take six months to produce. Every volume was painstakingly written by hand, usually in Latin, by monks, who were among the small number of people at the time who could actually read and write. Most people never saw a book unless it was on display in a church.

The development of the printing press changed the role of books in society. The press was the world's first mass-production machine, and each one could produce about one hundred books a month. Within ten years of its invention, printing technology spread across Europe, and thousands of printers went into business in Germany, France, Italy, and Netherlands. The printers produced encyclopedic works, cheap manuals, religious writs, political pamphlets, calendars, posters, and even playing cards.

The increased availability of printed matter in the late 1450s occurred during the height of the Italian Renaissance. New books about the rebirth of art, music, and literature in Italy helped fuel interest in the Renaissance throughout northern Europe. In the 1470s an English merchant, writer, and diplomat named William Caxton took a keen interest in printing. In 1473, while living in Belgium, Caxton produced the first book ever published in English, a romance story called *Recuyell of the Historyes of Troye.*

Caxton returned to England in 1475 and set up a print shop in the central London neighborhood of Westminster. He specialized in printing encyclopedic collections about Renaissance science, history, art, and literature. Caxton's books were written in simple language that literate citizens could understand, and this brought him quick success.

By the early 1500s dozens of printers were operating in London. The availability of books sparked a revolution in literacy. By the mid-1500s over 66 percent of London's male servants and over 80 percent of its tradesmen could write at least well enough to sign their names. In rural areas less than 25 percent of adults possessed this skill. Among women the figures were not as high. Few women of any region or social class were literate. It is estimated that only about 10 percent of English-women could write their names during the sixteenth century.

By the time of Elizabeth's ascension to the throne, literacy had become a critical tool for those wishing to improve their financial and social standing. In Elizabethan society, as Renaissance scholar Louis B. Wright explains,

A vast number of upstarts were seeking to better their social conditions by rising to the rank above them or by increasing the dignity of the ranking [in] which they found themselves. Never before had there been such widespread zeal for knowledge, so great a return upon an investment in learning, such necessity for an acquaintance with a common stock of knowledge with which every intelligent man was expected to be reasonably familiar.[3]

William Caxton—merchant, diplomat, writer, and printer—reviews a publication printed on his press. Caxton was the first of many English printers who made books available to the English public, a feat that sparked a revolution in literacy.

Exploration in the New World

The printed word also played an important role in spreading information about discoveries in the New World. In 1492 Christopher Columbus had sailed from Spain to the Bahamas—the first European explorer known to reach the Americas. After Columbus's historical journey, dozens of pamphlets and books about the adventure were sold throughout Europe.

By the early 1500s the Italian explorer and mapmaker Amerigo Vespucci was as famous as Columbus. Vespucci sailed between Spain and the eastern coast of South America several times between 1499 and 1504, charting 6,000 miles (9,656km) of the South American coast. Vespucci published his travel journals in 1505, and the books were read with delight by Europeans eager for accounts of the exotic new lands. In 1507 German mapmaker Martin Waldseemüller printed Vespucci's map of the New World and labeled it "America" in the explorer's honor.

Columbus, Vespucci, and others were not initially searching for new lands. They were sailing west from Europe in hopes of finding a shortcut to Asia. If such a route could be found, European traders could import silks, spices, and other valued goods from India and China without sailing around the dangerous seas at the southernmost tip of the African continent. However, the North American continent lay between Europe and Asia, a fact that was not initially known by the Europeans.

The king and queen of Spain sponsored Columbus and Vespucci, and the explorers claimed the New World entirely and exclusively for Spain. In England this was viewed as a threat by King Henry VII, who ascended the throne in 1485. Henry wanted to limit Spanish claims on the New World while opening up new trade routes for England. In 1497 the king hired his own Italian navigator and explorer, John Cabot, to find a sea route to the Indies and China.

Despite Henry's efforts, the Spanish proved to be formidable enemies in the booming age of discovery. Spanish ships called carracks were better suited for sailing long distances than the barge-like English ships. Carracks had four masts with a new type of triangular sail that allowed seamen to make the most efficient use of the winds. The Spanish ships also had sturdy hulls that allowed them to withstand the rough waters of the Atlantic Ocean.

With its powerful ships and ruthless conquistadores, Spain transformed the New World. In 1519 conquistador Hernán Cortés and a small group of soldiers slaughtered the indigenous Aztec natives in Mexico and looted their vast treasures of gold, silver, and jewels. In 1520 the conquistador Francisco Pizarro established a Spanish presence in South America, conquering the indigenous Incas in Peru in 1532.

Treasure Fleets and Pirates

By the 1540s Spain controlled a New World empire, called the Spanish Main. The Spanish territory included most of the islands in the Caribbean Sea, much of present-day Florida, Texas, Mexico, and Central America, and the northern and eastern coasts of South America. The Spanish Main supplied Spain with valuable resources, including spices, hardwoods, hides, silver, gold, and gems. Spain used this wealth to assemble the largest, best-equipped army and navy in Europe.

The riches of the Spanish Main were transported back to Spain twice a year on treasure fleets dominated by a new kind of ship. The multidecked Spanish galleon was bigger, faster, and even more agile than the carrack. However, the treasure fleets were vulnerable to French pirates, called privateers. Unlike pirates who robbed and plundered for their own personal gain, the privateers operated with a special license, called a letter of marque and reprisal. This official document was signed by the French king Francis I. Whoever possessed a letter of marque had permission to attack and capture vessels belonging to Spain and other enemies of France. Privateers were expected to turn over most of their loot to the king but were allowed to retain a portion for their efforts.

Catherine of Aragon and Prince Arthur

In the early days of New World exploration and piracy, the English monarchs were consumed with matters closer to home. After Henry VII died in 1509, his son, Henry VIII, became king of England. Shortly

The Renaissance

The term *renaissance* is French for rebirth and is used to describe the flowering of arts, literature, music, and architecture that began in Italy in the late 1300s and reached England in the mid-1500s. On the European continent the Renaissance was characterized by advancements in architecture, painting, and sculpture techniques. In England the Renaissance was most influential in the fields of science and literature.

The roots of the artistic Renaissance were in a movement called humanism, which encouraged people to realize their capabilities as individuals and to express their personal thoughts and beliefs through the arts. This stood in contrast to pre-Renaissance philosophy, in which great value was given to a life of quiet contemplation and religious devotion. Renaissance humanism elevated modern concepts like individualism, nationalism, secularism, and capitalism. In England humanism was behind the move toward literacy and learning, in which people actively sought self-improvement and economic advancement through reading, writing, and studying. Playwright William Shakespeare reflected humanist values in his works, which depicted kings, aristocrats, and religious authorities as people with human failings rather than godlike powers.

During the Renaissance, kings, queens, and aristocrats commissioned great works of public art and built gilded churches, ornamental theaters, and decorative government buildings and universities. By the time the Renaissance ended in the 1600s, the way Europeans perceived the world was permanently transformed by Renaissance master artists like Leonardo da Vinci and Michelangelo and by English writers like Shakespeare.

after ascending the throne, Henry VIII wedded the Spanish princess Catherine of Aragon. This marriage, and what followed, changed the course of English history and ultimately led to Elizabeth's ascension to the throne.

The events that led to the marriage of Henry and Catherine began in 1486 with the birth of Henry's older brother, Arthur Tudor. When Arthur turned one, his father, Henry VII, began searching for a suitable bride for Arthur, who would one day be crowned king of England. Recognizing the rising power of Spain, Henry VII chose Catherine of Aragon to be his son's wife. Such a marriage would cement a political alliance with her parents, King Ferdinand and Queen Isabella of Spain. Catherine's substantial dowry of silver and gold also appealed to Henry VII, who was desperately short of money. Negotiations lasted more than a decade before the two sides finally agreed to the marriage.

The marriage between Catherine, 16, and Arthur, 15, took place in London in 1501. Within six months of the wedding, however, Arthur was dead—killed by an unknown disease. While the marriage was short, it had long-lasting consequences. Henry VII was obligated to return Catherine's dowry, and he did not want to do so. Within hours of his son's death, Henry VII was making plans for his second son, ten-year-old Prince Henry, to marry Catherine.

The Brother's Wife

Once again Henry VII entered into marriage negotiations with Ferdinand and Isabella, but a religious concern threatened the arrangement. At the time, Catholicism was the official religion of all European nations, including England and Spain. The pope in Rome was head of the Catholic Church and, as such, he was the final authority on all religious matters, including the legitimacy of a Christian marriage. So although Europe's rulers acted according to their own needs and the needs of their countries, they often found it necessary to seek the blessing of the pope for actions of public importance—such as a marriage.

Tudor England

Henry VII wanted the pope's blessing for Prince Henry to marry Catherine. However, a passage in the Bible's book of Leviticus (20:16) states that a man cannot marry his brother's widow: "If a man shall take his brother's wife, it is an impurity; he hath uncovered his brother's

The Spread of Schools

In the decades leading up to the Elizabethan era, those who could read and write held a higher status in society. In order to satisfy the demand for literacy, a large number of schools opened in London during the early 1500s. Boys attended these schools from 7:00 a.m. to 7:00 p.m., with a two-hour break for lunch and hours of additional study in the evening. Prayers were recited three times a day, and classes were conducted in English, Latin, Greek, and Hebrew.

Many schools had primitive dormitories, where students lived in primitive conditions. At Westminster Abbey, students resided in an unheated stone building that once had been used to store grain. The school day began with prayers in Latin at 5:00 a.m., and students were expected to study in their chambers until midnight. Those who failed to follow orders, bathe properly, and study hard were subjected to flogging with a birch stick or cane. British historian Liz Picard describes the punishment meted out to students at Westminster Abbey: "William Udall, who was appointed High Master . . . had already made a name for himself at Eton [College] as an enthusiastic flogger, to which he subjected any boy not neatly dressed, hands and nails clean, hair combed and free of nits."

Liza Picard, *Elizabeth's London.* New York: St. Martin's, 2003, p. 197.

nakedness; they shall be childless." Catherine claimed that Leviticus did not apply to her brief marriage to Arthur because the marriage was never consummated due to his poor health. Henry VII presented this information to Pope Julius II and asked that he issue a papal dispensation. This document would annul the marriage of Arthur and Catherine and allow her betrothal to young Henry. The pope granted the king's request and gave his blessing to the marriage in 1504.

Upsetting the Great Chain of Being

Henry VII died in April 1509, and Henry VIII, who had just turned eighteen, ascended the throne within days. He soon proposed to Catherine, and the couple wedded on June 11, 1509. Catherine was crowned queen of England about two weeks later.

The union of Henry and Catherine was troubled from the start. Henry was desperate to produce a male heir, and Catherine seemed unable to do so. During the first five years of marriage, Catherine gave birth to a stillborn baby, had a miscarriage, and gave birth to two boys who died soon after. Finally, in 1516 the queen gave birth to a healthy daughter named Mary. In the two years that followed, Catherine suffered through several more miscarriages and stillbirths.

By 1525 Catherine was forty years old, and Henry was convinced he would never have a son to take his place on the throne. At the time the idea of Princess Mary succeeding Henry was seen as a violation of a widely accepted concept known as the Great Chain of Being. This belief posited that every object in the universe had a place on a great chain that extended to heaven. God sat atop the chain, followed by angels, humans, animals, plants, metals, stones, and elements like fire and water. In regard to humans, the English king sat atop the chain and was said to be God's representative on Earth. To disobey the king was to disobey God. Average men were below the king on the chain, and women and children were beneath them.

Henry believed that if Mary ascended the throne, it would violate the Great Chain of Being. As history professors Robert Bucholz and Newton Key explain: "If God was male, and the king his representative on earth, how could a woman represent Him or wield His power? If God had placed man at the head of the State, the Church, and the family, what would be the consequences for the Chain, *for Order itself*, in yielding that position to a woman?"[4]

The King's Great Matter

While pondering the meaning of the Great Chain of Being, Henry began to doubt his religious beliefs. When speaking to his advisors, the king wondered aloud if God was punishing or cursing him by denying him a son. Ultimately, Henry decided he needed a new queen to produce a legitimate male heir. Within the royal court, this problem was referred to as the king's *great matter*.

Around 1526 the king became infatuated with Anne Boleyn and likely saw a solution to his great matter. The nineteen-year-old Anne was the daughter of Tom Boleyn, a royal courtier and diplomat. She was sister to Mary Boleyn, one of Henry's mistresses. Anne was highly educated, spoke French and Latin fluently, sang, danced, and was knowledgeable about Renaissance art, music, and literature. Although she was not viewed as the most beautiful woman of the court, she was charismatic, polished, and cultured. According to Tudor historian Derek Wilson, Henry was smitten: "Anne brought into Henry's life that combination of youthful charm and mature sophistication that Catherine possessed no longer. . . . Like Catherine, Anne was strong-minded [and] Henry liked to have people around him who were clear-thinking and intelligent—provided they were tactful enough not to show him up. He enjoyed debate, particularly religious debate."[5]

If Henry wanted religious debate, he would have it. The king desperately wanted to marry Anne, but divorce was strictly forbidden by the Catholic church. Henry needed the pope to intercede once again to annul his marriage to Catherine. The king's strategy was to reverse the 1504 papal dispensation that allowed him to marry Catherine in the first place. Henry claimed that Catherine had actually consummated her marriage with Arthur and therefore had violated the law as stated in Leviticus when she and Henry wedded.

The king's chief advisor, Thomas Cromwell, negotiated unsuccessfully with the church for years. Meanwhile, Anne became pregnant with Henry's child in late 1532. In January 1533 the two married. On June 1 Anne was named queen consort, a title given to a spouse who was not descended from royalty. On September 7, 1533, Anne gave birth to a daughter, Elizabeth, the future queen of England.

England Moves Toward Protestantism

A new pope, Clement VII, claimed Henry's marriage to Anne was illegal and threatened him with excommunication (expulsion from the church). Henry responded by moving England toward Protestantism, a religion founded by German monk Martin Luther in 1517. Luther established Protestantism to protest what he viewed as the corrupt practices of the Catholic Church. Luther was excommunicated for his beliefs in 1520, but the religion he founded quickly gained followers. During an era called the Protestant Reformation, Protestantism was adopted by princes in Germany and gained popularity in Switzerland, Denmark, Norway, and Sweden.

Protestantism was introduced to England by Henry VIII beginning in 1534 with a series of laws, or acts, approved by England's governing body, Parliament. The Act of Supremacy officially stripped the pope of his religious authority and named Henry the "only supreme head in earth of the Church of England."[6] To dispute this claim was an act of treason punishable by hanging or burning at the stake. Other laws were passed that allowed the king to supersede the pope and the church in all matters of religion and justice. Initially, there was strong opposition to Henry's religious revolution, but all dissent was brutally suppressed through the use of torture and public executions.

The Beheading of Anne Boleyn

Even as religious issues roiled his kingdom, Henry began to question his marriage to Anne. The king viewed his new wife as opinionated, irritable, and temperamental. This might have been overlooked if she had given birth to a male heir, but like Catherine before her, Anne produced only a daughter, followed by several miscarriages and stillbirths.

Henry was not willing to wait any longer. Rather than seek a divorce, the king devised a sinister plan to rid himself of his wife. In April 1536 Cromwell accused Anne of having romantic affairs with five young men of her court, including her brother, George. Historians have long agreed that the charges against Anne were false. Nevertheless, two weeks later the queen was tried and convicted of adultery,

King Henry VIII enjoys a flirtatious moment with Anne Boleyn as Queen Catherine peers anxiously around a doorway. Henry eventually divorced Catherine and married Anne. The child of their union, Elizabeth, carried on the Tudor name.

incest, and high treason and sentenced to death. On May 17, 1536, her marriage to Henry was declared null and void. On May 19 Anne was beheaded along with the five purported male adulterers.

Elizabeth was only two years and eight months old when her mother was executed. Henry claimed that the child had been born out of wedlock since he was not married to Anne when Elizabeth was conceived. This meant Elizabeth was illegitimate, which denied her the title of princess. Despite this stain on her name, Elizabeth was treated well. She was raised and educated like a princess by sympathetic royal governesses.

The day after Anne's death, Henry became engaged to his new mistress, Jane Seymour. They were married on May 30. In October 1537 Queen Jane gave Henry what he had wanted for nearly thirty years: a son. However, the baby, named Edward, was only twelve days old when Jane died from complications of the birth.

Elizabeth Is Crowned

Henry married three more women before his death at age fifty-five in 1547. He was succeeded by Edward VI, his nine-year-old son with Jane. Edward was raised a Protestant and, despite his age, took a keen interest in religious matters. With Edward's encouragement, Protestantism became firmly established in England.

Edward died of illness in 1553 at age fifteen, having been the king of England for little more than six years. His successor, Mary I, was the daughter of Henry and Catherine. Mary was married to King Philip II of Spain, and both were staunch Catholics. Mary moved to reestablish Catholicism in England by repealing the religious laws instituted by Henry. The queen ordered nearly three hundred Protestant leaders burned at the stake, which earned her the nickname "Bloody Mary."

When Mary died at age forty-two in 1558, her half sister, Elizabeth, ascended the throne. Most English citizens viewed the new queen only as the illegitimate daughter of Henry VIII and Anne Boleyn. Few had hopes that twenty-five-year-old Elizabeth could rise to greatness. England had many problems at the time. The country was divided over religion, Spain's power continued to grow, and the future looked uncertain for the young, inexperienced queen.

Chapter 2

Rich and Poor in England

Eleven days after Elizabeth I became queen of England on November 17, 1558, a grand procession began a winding journey 20 miles (32km) from the Tudor palace in Hatfield to London. The new queen, with her reddish-blond hair framing her face, rode in a plush carriage at the head of a cavalcade that contained one thousand nobles, government officials, and relatives. Along the way the young queen held meetings with foreign ambassadors, English judges, and religious leaders. On November 28 Elizabeth's entourage rolled into London, where the lord mayor presented the new queen with a purse containing one thousand gold coins. Then the queen spoke to the assembled crowd: "Be ye ensured that I will be as good to you as ever [a] Queen was unto her people. . . . And persuade yourselves that for the safety and quietness of you all I will not spare if need be to spend my blood."[7]

The splendid procession continued to the royal palace and fortress known as the Tower of London. The Tower was an impregnable fort that housed the stately living quarters of kings and queens. It was also home to England's most infamous prison. Now as Elizabeth approached the Tower in an open chariot, cannons fired celebratory volleys.

The coronation of Elizabeth I took place on January 15, 1559, at Westminster Abbey. The day before the official ceremony, Elizabeth once again rode through the streets of London. Historian A.N. Wilson describes the scene: "She was dressed in a cloth-of-gold robe. Her hair streamed over her shoulders. On her head she wore a small circlet of gold. She sat on cloth-of-gold cushions and a rich, satin-lined litter, open at all sides with a canopy at the top, carried by the four barons of [Kent and Sussex]."[8]

Elizabeth's coronation was one of the most elaborate ceremonies in English history up to that time. The grand spectacle began on January 14, 1558, with a daylong coronation parade through London. Thousands of officials, aristocrats, and soldiers rode expensive carriages through the crowd-lined streets. The queen arrived on a golden litter. The next day she was officially crowned at Westminster Abbey as church bells rang and crowds cheered in the streets.

At a time when most people earned only pennies a week, the extraordinary celebration stood in marked contrast to the lives of most of Elizabeth's subjects. Although the queen's reign is remembered as a golden time of literature, commerce, and exploration, during the Elizabethan era the vast majority of people in England were poor, illiterate peasants. They worked from dawn to dark and lived much like their ancestors had lived for hundreds of years.

Country Life

In the second half of the sixteenth century, over 90 percent of England's people lived in rural areas under a feudal system first put into place around the eleventh century. Land was equal to wealth, and the countryside was divided up among a few rich nobles, each referred to as the lord of the manor. The lords owned large tracts of farmland, woodland, pastures filled with sheep, and even entire villages. Lords lived in large manor houses and allowed landless, unskilled peasants to occupy one-room, thatched-roof houses on their lands. The peasants worked for the lord of the manor in exchange for protection, justice, and the right to farm a few acres of land. Skilled laborers, such as blacksmiths, carpenters, and artisans, rented their shops from the lord of the manor.

In the English countryside larger villages had only five or six streets. Each one held a weekly or biweekly street market called a "cheap," where people could purchase clothing, dishes, and foods, such as apples, cheese, and bread. Like every other aspect of rural Elizabethan life, the markets were regulated by and operated with the permission of the local lord of the manor.

Elizabeth is crowned as England's new queen in a ceremony at Westminster Abbey on January 15, 1559. The days before and after the coronation were marked by elaborate and costly parades and celebrations.

Crowds and Traffic

At the time of Elizabeth's coronation, only 8 percent of English people lived in towns with populations of more than 5,000. However, the feudal system began to break down during Elizabethan times as thousands of peasants left the countryside to search for better opportunities in London. Historians estimate that in 1520, the city was home to about 50,000 people. By 1600 that number had grown to around 250,000. (England's second-largest city, Norwich, had about 20,000 people in 1600.)

Although the number of people in London expanded, the city's borders did not. The population was packed into a roughly 1-square-mile (2.6 sq. km) area fronted by the Thames River and surrounded by ancient walls on the other three sides.

The Thames was London's main transportation artery and was crowded with thousands of barges, ferries, rowboats, and sailboats. Along the river shores, fishers cast lines and spread nets to pull in shad, salmon, flounder, sturgeon, and shrimp. Workers called watermen were the taxi drivers of the era, transporting customers upstream, downstream, or across the river for a fee. Those who did not wish to pay could cross the Thames on London Bridge, which led to the growing village of Southwark on the southern bank of the river.

Most of London's crooked, narrow cobblestone streets were originally medieval footpaths. They were packed with teams of horses pulling all manner of carts, wagons, and carriages. As a Venetian traveler noted in the 1560s, Londoners "often use carts pulled by two, four, six, or more horses . . . the carters go whistling behind to urge them along."[9] These vehicles had no brakes, and pedestrians who got in the way were often crushed beneath their wheels. Traffic jams were common and sometimes caused by gruesome Elizabethan justice. British historian Liza Picard explains:

> You might equally meet men or women being whipped through the city, their backs raw and bloody, or a criminal being [transported in a caged cart] or you might see a petty criminal in the stocks or pillory withstanding a rain of mud and missiles. And

you might decide to take another route altogether if you found that your intended way passed under a gateway with part of a rotting human body on it.[10]

Tudor Homes

For those who could afford it, a sturdy home provided refuge from the chaos in the streets. The homes of average Londoners were low-roofed wood, brick, or stone buildings two or three stories in height. They often hung over narrow streets and alleys, where the upper floors almost met, blocking out any view of the sun and sky.

Wealthier citizens lived on wide lanes lined with timber-framed homes built in what is now known as the Tudor style. These structures were constructed from a series of oak beam frames and cross members. As London's population surged, many Tudor homes were subdivided into a maze of small apartments. These crowded places might house several dozen people, all sharing a single toilet, or privy. And there were thousands who could not even afford to rent a room in an overcrowded tenement. These people lived in crude shanties made from wood scraps, dirt, and animal hides. The shacks were packed into any available open space. Some were even squeezed between the buttresses, or outer stone supports, of the renowned St. Paul's Cathedral.

Water and Sewage

One of life's most important commodities, water, was delivered to Londoners through an elaborate system of pipes, conduits, and waterwheels. Channeled in from rivers and springs outside the city walls, the water was available for free at public fountains. (Although the city is located on the Thames River, the water was undrinkable because it was salty and extremely polluted.)

While sixteenth-century engineers were able to deliver fresh water, they had no means of dealing with the steady stream of sewage produced by the large population. In dirty, overcrowded neighborhoods, such as Shoreditch, Cripplegate, and St. Savior's, people tossed the contents of their chamber pots out of windows and sometimes from the

Unwholesome London

For the majority of its citizens, London was an extremely un-healthy place. The presence of polluted water, raw sewage, bad food, and other filth attracted rats, lice, fleas, flies, and other pests that spread diseases. A report by the College of Physicians in the early 1600s listed the following "annoyances" that fostered disease and death:

> [Residents of city buildings] by whom the houses were so pestered [full of lice] that they became unwholesome; neglect of cleansing of common sewers and town ditches; and permitting standing ponds in diverse inns; unclean-liness of the streets; the [cattle pens] so near the City, especially on the north side; the slaughter-houses in the City; burying of infected people in the churches and churchyards of the City . . . the selling of musty [barley] corn in the public markets; bakers baking unwholesome corn; butchers killing unsound cattle; tainted fish.

Quoted in F.P. Wilson, *The Plague in Shakespeare's London*. Oxford: Oxford University Press, 1963, pp. 23–24.

upper floors of apartments. Raw sewage flowed through the streets and ditches. Open spaces were piled with garbage that might include food refuse, medical waste, parts of dead animals from slaughterhouses, and even human remains.

"In Time of Plague"

Life was short for those who lived in and around the filth of the city. In the poorest areas of London, historians say, the average man lived to his mid-twenties. In the middle-class neighborhoods where merchants, scholars, and government officials resided, men could expect to live an extra ten years on average. Within the walls of castles, palaces, and mansions, the wealthiest men could expect to live to see their fiftieth birthdays. On average, women were considered old if they lived past forty years of age. Elizabeth was much older than most of her subjects when she died in 1603 at age sixty-nine.

Regardless of social class, few people expected to live a long time. Young men were killed by war, women routinely died during childbirth, and infant mortality rates were high. Regular droughts, storms, and crop failures resulted in widespread starvation in the countryside. The biggest killer, the bubonic plague, or Black Death, periodically wiped out up to one-third of the population.

The plague was caused by disease-carrying fleas that lived on black rats. Infected fleas often jumped onto humans and bit them. When this occurred the microscopic bacterium that causes the plague entered the bloodstream. Within hours the lymph glands in the groin, neck, and armpits swelled with large, black, oozing lumps called buboes. Two-thirds of those infected died within a week.

The plague originated in Central Asia and first arrived in Europe in October 1347, when it reached Italy. In the following months the Black Death spread north across Europe, reaching England in July 1348. During the four years that followed, about 50 percent of the population on the European continent—an estimated 100 million people—died from the plague. In England the death toll was lower, with about 20 percent of the population dying from the plague. Whatever the exact figures, the Black Death reappeared periodically throughout Europe for centuries.

The proliferation of rats in London made the city particularly vulnerable to the bubonic plague. During the Elizabethan era, 1563 was one of the worst years for the plague; about twenty thousand people died from the illness—more than a quarter of London's population. Other bad plague years included 1591 and 1603. While the rich often fled London during epidemics, the plague did not respect social class. In 1600 writer Thomas Nash made this point in his poem "In Time of Plague":

Rich men, trust not in wealth,
Gold cannot buy you health;
Physic himself must fade;
All things to end are made;
The plague full swift goes by;
I am sick, I must die.
Lord have mercy on us.[11]

"Everlasting Lodgings"

As plague swept through the country, bodies piled up everywhere, forcing officials to search for ways to dispose of them quickly. Corpses of plague victims were wrapped in cloth called winding sheets and thrown without burial rites into mass graves called "pest pits." Poet Thomas Dekker described the bleak situation: "The dead were tumbled into their everlasting lodgings (ten in one heape, and twenty in another). . . . The gallant and the beggar lay together; the scholar and the carter in one bed."[12]

The plague was but one killer during the Elizabethan era. People also died quickly after contracting typhus, which is spread by lice and fleas. Other diseases such as tuberculosis, syphilis, scurvy, and malaria killed countless thousands. Smallpox, which was prevalent in London, wiped out thousands from time to time. Elizabeth contracted smallpox in 1562 but quickly recovered. Others were not so lucky. Lady Sidney, who nursed the queen back to health, contracted the disease and, like thousands of smallpox survivors on the streets of London, was permanently disfigured from the fluid-filled blisters that erupted all over her body.

The Revolution of 1559

Even as death, disease, and disorder swept through England, religion remained a central pillar in peoples' lives. However, like many other aspects of Elizabethan England, matters of religion were unsettled and sometimes chaotic. Before Elizabeth ascended the throne, her

half sister, Mary I, had reversed Henry VIII's moves toward Protestantism along with repealing the Act of Supremacy passed by Parliament. During Mary's five-year reign, all English citizens were required to practice Catholicism. Unlike Mary, Elizabeth was Protestant—and she intended to settle the religious issue once and for all.

When Parliament assembled for the first time under Elizabeth's reign, it approved two acts put forth by the queen that were later described as the Revolution of 1559. The Act of Supremacy of 1559 spelled out its significance in its full title: "An Act restoring to the Crown the ancient jurisdiction over the state ecclesiastical and spiritual, and abolishing all foreign power repugnant to the same."[13] In simple language this meant that the Queen was restored as the head of the church, which was now declaring its independence from the pope in Rome.

The Act of Supremacy included ten sections of dense legal jargon. One section required all religious officials, teachers, and university graduates to swear an oath. They were required to say the queen was the only supreme governmental, spiritual, and religious ruler of the realm.

The second part of the Elizabethan religious revolution was called the Act of Uniformity. In 1559 the act made the English Book of Common Prayer the official prayer book of the Anglican Communion (national churches). This book, originally published during the reign of Edward VI, established Protestant rituals and rites and was used to replace Catholic prayer books. Divergence from the Book of Common Prayer, or objections to it, could be punished by life imprisonment. Another part of the Act of Uniformity required all men to go to church once a week or face a fine of twelve shillings, about twenty-five dollars.

In order to enforce the new laws, Elizabeth issued a series of commands. Every preacher was required to give a quarterly sermon reminding his flock that the queen was the highest power under God. Every parish was required to make available to the congregation a Bible written in

Daily activities take place in the small apartments and ground-floor business depicted in this painting of a subdivided Tudor home.

English and a copy of the Book of Common Prayer. All Catholic shrines and paintings were to be destroyed so thoroughly that no memories of them would remain. This proclamation resulted in the destruction of thousands of priceless altars, statues, stained-glass windows, and paintings, which were burned, smashed, or covered with whitewash.

Elizabeth's laws and injunctions were part of what was called the Elizabethan Religious Settlement. Protestantism was established, and the pope's authority, Catholic mass, and monasteries were banned. The laws were by no means supported by all, and members of Parliament engaged in protracted, bitter debate over the provisions. However, in the years that followed 1559, most people in England accepted Protestantism, and religious issues were settled for the most part.

Dire Poverty

Before England's Protestant Reformation, the poor were clothed, fed, and otherwise cared for by monks in Catholic monasteries. Henry VIII upset the system when he shut down the monasteries and appropriated their wealth in the late 1530s. In the decades that followed, England's poor were left on their own at a time when their numbers were growing every year. Even with the plague and other diseases killing thousands, England had a high birth rate, and its population steadily increased during the Elizabethan era.

With more workers available, wages fell. More people meant more demand for food and housing, which in turn led to a spike in food prices and rents. By the 1580s about one-third of England's population lived in dire poverty. An estimated forty thousand people were homeless, wandering the countryside in search of seasonal employment. These people included military veterans, beggars, the disabled, the sick, and criminals. The situation led writer John Howe in 1582 to pose the question, "Was there ever, in any age, the like number of poor people as there are in the present, begging in the streets of the City and wandering the fields so idly, being ready to attempt mischief upon any light occasion?"[14]

The poor were seen as a threat to society and subjected to cruel punishments. In 1547 Parliament passed a law requiring the letter *V*

Shopping at the Cheap

Centuries before the invention of electricity and refrigerators, Londoners purchased fresh food, such as beef, fish, fowl, fruit, and vegetables at "cheaps," the old English word for marketplaces.

Farmers drove sheep, cattle, and pigs though London streets to slaughterhouses in Eastcheap, where butchers killed the animals to be sold. The Stocks Market was home to twenty-five fishmongers, who sold all manner of fish and seafood. Flower and root sellers worked the stalls of Cornhill and Cheap, and Gracechurch Street was known for its dairy, pork, and vegetable products. Fruit and grain farmers from the countryside worked the Queenhithe market, on the banks of the Thames. At Smithfield live animals were sold on Wednesdays and Fridays.

Markets were generally open six days a week between 6:00 a.m. and 5:00 p.m., but some operated every day and sold after dark by candlelight. In addition to the "cheaps," there were numerous small shops that specialized in selling cheeses, spices, salt and sugar, and baked goods, such as bread, pies, and fruit tarts. Proprietors of such shops often lived in apartments located above their stores.

for vagrant to be branded with a hot iron onto the chest of anyone who refused to work. Other penalties for being poor included whipping, imprisonment, enslavement, deportation, and hanging. Some towns rejected such punishments, but others did not. In Middlesex there seemed to be great enthusiasm for penalizing people simply for being poor. Between 1572 and 1575 Middlesex authorities branded forty-four vagrants, forced eight into slavery, and hanged five.

Enacting Poor Laws

Despite such statistics, most English citizens of the Elizabethan era believed that the "deserving poor," those who could not work due to their health, age, or other circumstances, should receive help. In 1563 and 1572, in order to help the deserving poor, Parliament passed a series of acts known as the Poor Laws.

The Poor Laws made poverty a local responsibility. The justice of the peace in each county was required to collect a tax, called a poor rate, from local lords of the manor. The poor rate was spent on food, clothing, housing, and medical care for the deserving poor. In larger cities governments organized special care for orphans, the old, and the sick. In addition, members of some wealthy families believed it was their religious duty to help children. They paid for orphans to attend school or learn a trade.

The vagrants who were not deserving poor but were simply unemployed were forced to live in workhouses. Women in these institutions were required to spin wool and make clothing. Men were put to work forging iron. The workhouse experience was meant to be unpleasant in order to force the poor back into society. Wives were separated from husbands. Children were separated from their parents and sent to orphanages or placed in apprentice programs.

The problems of the Elizabethan poor were addressed once again with the 1597 Act for the Relief of the Poor. This system nationalized the collection of the poor rate, making it the duty of the national government. A bureaucrat called the overseer of the poor determined how much money was needed, set the poor rate, collected the money, and distributed it. The act also authorized parishes to build houses for the homeless and provide schooling for impoverished children.

Even as the rich and poor formed the basis for Elizabethan society, the English economy was changing. London attracted merchants and traders from across Europe, which transformed it into one of the most sophisticated and successful cities in the world. While life might have been brutal and short for many, the Elizabethans were building the foundation for a modern nation whose power and wealth would dominate the world for centuries.

Chapter 3

The Elizabethan Renaissance

In 1599 a Swiss tourist named Thomas Platter wrote, "This city of London is not only brimful of curiosities, but so popular also that one simply cannot walk along the streets for the crowd."[15] Among the people packing London's busy streets, Platter noticed a large number of newcomers rarely seen in his native country. Due to a booming economic system and a reputation for religious tolerance, sixteenth-century London was a magnet for people from Spain, Italy, France, Germany, and Netherlands. There was also a mix of races and religions, including Jews from the European continent and African Muslims.

Immigrants, referred to as strangers, were often a source of controversy and complaint among English natives. Strangers were condemned for packing into overcrowded apartments, relying on government relief, refusing to learn English, and taking jobs from natives. Foreigners were also blamed for spreading the plague, smallpox, and other diseases.

Despite the criticism, immigrants made lasting contributions to Elizabethan culture, which was experiencing rapid growth in art, science, and literature. The Venetian glassmaker Jacob Verselyn (sometimes spelled Verzellini) set up what was called a glasshouse in London in 1575. Verselyn changed the way glass was made, using soda ash from seaweed. This gave his drinking glasses a unique brown tint. Verselyn operated with an exclusive patent, granted by Queen Elizabeth I, who was one of the chief buyers of his beautiful Renaissance-style glass.

Other immigrants who operated with exclusive patents included the German Diricke (or Derrick) Anthony, the chief engraver at the royal mint. Anthony oversaw the production of stamps, money, and official documents. Less renowned immigrant artisans in London included Belgian diamond cutters, French hatmakers, and Italian perfumers.

Painters to the Tudors

London's most influential foreigners were northern European Renaissance painters, who created large, finely detailed oil portraits of royals, courtiers, and aristocrats. The artists were from Germany, Netherlands, northern France, and Flanders, an area of present-day Belgium. They brought a high-quality Renaissance style of painting to England during an era when native artistic innovation was at a historic low. The dearth of good English painters was the result of a war waged on religious art by Tudor rulers.

During the early sixteenth century, most English art was based on Catholic religious themes, such as dramatic paintings of the saints and of Jesus on the cross. During the English Reformation, Henry VIII and other Protestant leaders deemed these images sacrilegious. As Hugh Latimer, Bishop of Worcester, wrote in 1536, religious images "are to be put out of the church. . . . It is against God's commandment that Christian men should make curtsey or reverence to the image of Our Savior."[16]

As the Reformation took hold in England, churches were violently stripped of what was described as heretical imagery. Stained-glass windows were shattered, intricately carved pews were smashed, gold and silver ornaments were melted down, large murals were painted over with whitewash, and even decorative gravestones were broken into pieces.

The destruction of religious art denied English artists a major source of income. Elsewhere in Europe, painters and sculptors received large commissions from numerous religious institutions to create work that glorified God. In England artists were employed primarily by royals and aristocrats. This led to a nearly exclusive focus on portraits created to lionize the wealthy and powerful.

The most influential portrait artist in England was from Augsburg, in present-day Germany. The printer and portrait artist Hans Holbein the Younger created tiny portraits called miniatures and large, life-sized portraits. Between 1536 and 1540 Holbein painted some of the most famous portraits of Henry VIII.

Holbein's 1537 full-length, 8-foot-high (2.4m) portrait of Henry is startling in its detail. It shows the bejeweled king in an aggressive stance, seeming virile, tall, and muscular. His chest is puffed out, his fists clenched, and he seems to be reaching for a dagger. However, Henry bore little resemblance to the man in the painting. In reality the king was aged, obese, and in ill health, and his legs were covered with open sores due to a medical condition. The painting was obviously propaganda, created to present Henry as an imposing and invincible monarch.

Portraits of Elizabeth I

Like her father, Elizabeth appreciated skillfully painted propaganda. She was famously sensitive about her likeness and strictly censored unauthorized pubic images. In the later decades of her reign, Elizabeth limited her royal patronage to a very small number of favored portraitists. These artists always made her look young, beautiful, and powerful despite her graying hair and aging features.

One of the queen's favorite painters, Nicholas Hilliard, excelled in miniature painting, a skill known as limning. Hilliard studied under Holbein and acknowledged his teacher in a 1570s pamphlet: "Holbein's manner of limning I have ever imitated, and hold it for the best."[17]

Miniature painters work with watercolors and create images on a surface of animal skin parchment called vellum. Hilliard created hundreds of fine portraits of Elizabethan courtiers on a miniature scale. Most were worn around the neck, inside lockets.

One of Hilliard's most renowned portraits of the queen was not a miniature but an oil painting known as *The Pelican Portrait*. This work, about 31 by 24 inches (78.5cm by 61cm), was created around 1574 when the queen was forty-one. It portrays Elizabeth in a formal, stylized manner. The queen is wearing a brooch displaying a pelican, which elevated Elizabeth to the level of a religious icon. Viewers of the era understood that the pelican is a traditional symbol of Jesus. It was commonly (but

The regal Armada Portrait, *painted by George Gower in 1588, depicts Elizabeth as both youthful and powerful. The queen's pose, along with various objects in the painting, suggest a bright and prosperous future for England under Elizabeth I.*

wrongly) believed that pelicans feed their young on their own blood if no other food is available. In the portrait, Elizabeth is portrayed as a saintly mother figure who would gladly bleed to feed her people.

Ageless and Immortal

Elizabeth appointed the painter George Gower as her official royal artist in 1581. One of Gower's most famous paintings, the *Armada Portrait*, was painted in late 1588 to commemorate England's victory over Spain's powerful naval fleet, the Armada.

Gower's *Armada Portrait* was meant to enhance Elizabeth's power in the eyes of her subjects. Although she was fifty-five years old at the time, an advanced age for women of the era, the queen looks healthy and youthful, with a clear, unwrinkled complexion. Her sparkling eyes gaze symbolically into the distance, where she can see a bright and prosperous future. The queen's hand rests on a globe, an emblem of world domination. Behind the queen's head, two windows are shown. The arrival of the Spanish Armada is framed on the left, and the dark, smoking ruins of the defeated ships are shown on the right.

One of the last portraits made of Elizabeth before her death was painted in 1600 by Isaac Oliver, a student of Hilliard's. Even at this late date, when Elizabeth was in her late sixties and two years from death, this painting shows the queen as youthful, ageless, and immortal.

Plays at the Innyard

During the English Renaissance, the nation only produced about twenty renowned painters, a tiny number compared with Italy or Flanders. With few official commissions available, many painters worked in the theater. During the Elizabethan era theatrical productions were extremely popular, and most featured painted stages sets and elaborate costumes and props.

The first plays in the English language were medieval mysteries and comedies known as mummers. These were performed seasonally, on religious holidays, and by wandering bands of amateurs who sang and acted out scenes on street corners. By the time of Elizabeth's reign, mummers had evolved into five-act plays. Performances were originally held at innyards, open courtyards where horses were stabled. Innyards were located at inns, guesthouses where alcohol was served and rooms were provided for travelers.

James Burbage, a former actor, became the leading promoter of plays at innyards, such as London's Bull Inn and the Cross Keys Inn. Playgoers were charged a small fee, and profits were shared with inn owners. Acting troupes were made up entirely of men and boys who played all roles, both male and female. Before a performance, actors built temporary stages and set up seats for the crowds. After a play, actors cleaned up the food waste, broken beer glasses, and other garbage left behind by the audience.

Amphitheaters

A typical innyard play attracted up to five hundred people, and by the 1570s these performances had become the most popular social gatherings in London, attracting rich and poor, young and old. In 1576 Burbage's success enabled him to build the first London amphitheater, simply called The Theatre. Within a decade there were more than twelve amphitheaters, most outside the city walls of London.

Amphitheaters were larger than innyard venues. An amphitheater could hold from fifteen hundred to three thousand people. It was circular or octagonal in shape, about 100 feet (30.5m) in diameter, and surrounded by a structure made from timber, stone, nails, and plaster. The stage was set on one side of the amphitheater at the edge of an open yard. Yards were surrounded by galleries of seats that rose up three levels. Plays were most often staged during the day, and yards were open to the sky to allow light in. The gallery areas were covered with thatched roofs that helped ward off London's notoriously soggy weather.

Customers who paid one penny gained admission to the yard. In this area, audiences could view the stage up close, but they were forced to stand through the entire performance. Oftentimes rain and snow pelted the viewers in the yard. Those who wished to pay an extra penny gained admission to the hard, wooden benches in the gallery. The wealthiest patrons paid up to six pennies to sit in luxurious box seats called lord's rooms. These rooms had exclusive entrances, were located close to the stage, and were visited by actors and playwrights after the show.

Private Playhouses

Amphitheaters attracted large crowds in warm weather but were not suitable for London's long, wet winters. In order to bring actors and audiences in from the cold, producers built indoor theaters called playhouses.

Elizabethan Music

During the Elizabethan era, music was played by rich and poor alike. Music could be heard everywhere, drifting on the wind from farm fields and rising above the boisterous chatter in taverns. Music added drama to Sunday church services and brought comic relief to Shakespeare's plays. People played woodwind instruments, such as flutes, bagpipes, and the hautboy, an ancestor to the modern oboe. Popular stringed instruments included the violin, harp, lute, and cittern, a forerunner to the guitar. Percussionists beat on drums, tambourines, cymbals, and triangles. And the wealthiest members of society owned harpsichords, piano-like instruments with keyboards. Nearly every major church had a pipe organ, which was one of the most complex and sophisticated instruments of the day. The organ at Winchester Cathedral had four hundred pipes and could produce beautiful music as well as sounds imitating birdsong, warfare, barking dogs, and falling rain.

Elizabeth I was a patron of the arts who sponsored many composers. William Byrd was famous for his madrigals, songs that combined poetry and melody into what might be called Elizabethan pop music. Thomas Morley, another renowned writer of madrigals, was also a pioneer in ensemble music. In this era before symphony orchestras, Morley wrote pieces for ensembles called consorts, which consisted of two viols and a flute, lute, cittern, and bandora, or bass cittern.

With the introduction of playhouses, the theater business became a year-round enterprise. Although playhouses had fewer seats than amphitheaters, producers could charge higher prices, up to twenty-six pennies. Plays could be held in the evening, with stages lit by dozens of candles. During intermission, food and drinks were served. Because the playhouses were permanent venues, artists created beautiful scenery, which was stored and reused in numerous productions. With the improved indoor acoustics, audiences could better hear the words of the actors. This gave playwrights the opportunity to create poetic, intricate pieces.

Shakespeare Reinvents Theater

The most popular plays during the golden age of Elizabethan theater, which began in the early 1590s, were historical dramas about English kings. Plays like Shakespeare's three-part *Henry VI* (1591) and Christopher Marlowe's *Edward II* (1594) portrayed the vaunted rulers as flawed characters with typical human foibles. Marlowe and Shakespeare both based their works on historically accurate books, and many Elizabethans learned English history not from reading but from attending plays. The historical dramas depicted petty quarrels between powerful aristocrats and kings obsessed with minor grievances. The playwrights blamed royal incompetence for England's loss of several crucial military battles and the needless slaughter of brave soldiers.

The plots conceived by Shakespeare, Marlowe, and others resembled modern-day soap operas—the action was continuous and the romance scandalous. The Elizabethan public could not get enough of the tragic twists and dramatic turns that dominated the lives of their kings.

Although Marlowe wrote only one English history, Shakespeare produced a number of such plays before he stopped writing in 1613. His dramas included *Henry IV*, *Henry V*, *Richard III*, and *Henry VIII* While any playwright would long be remembered for such works of genius, it is the Shakespearian tragedies *Hamlet*, *Othello*, *Macbeth*, and *Romeo and Juliet* that have been most widely produced. Shakespeare's plays also include the comedies *Much Ado About Nothing*, *A Midsummer Night's Dream*, and *Twelfth Night*.

Whether writing comedy or drama, Shakespeare is credited with reinventing theater. In earlier times most productions followed rigid rules established in ancient Greece, where plays were either strictly dramas or comedies. With his desire to keep the masses entertained, Shakespeare injected humorous scenes into dark dramas, thus inventing comic relief. While Greek plays all took place on a single day in one place, Shakespeare bent this rule when it suited him. For example, the character Hamlet is a young student at the beginning of the play and thirty years old at the end. And while Shakespeare sometimes adhered to historical facts, he was also capable of muddling reality for poetic purposes. In *Julius Caesar*, which takes place in 44 BC, a ticking clock is mentioned about fourteen hundred years before the invention of mechanical clocks. In *Antony and Cleopatra* the Egyptian queen expresses

The Globe Theatre, depicted in this twentieth-century illustration, was the most famous Elizabethan playhouse. Plays performed in playhouses such as the Globe made use of elaborate scenery and improved acoustics.

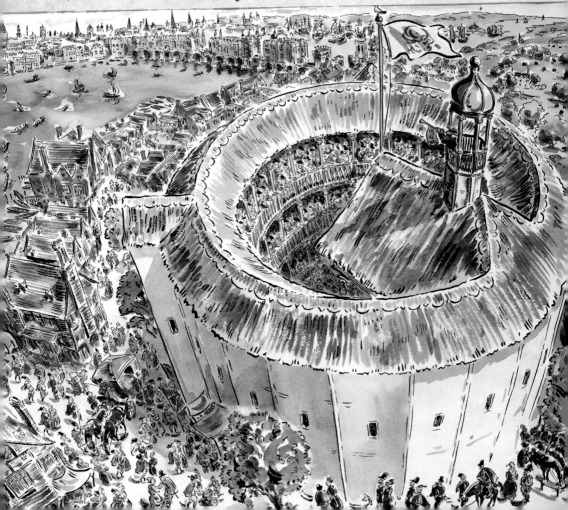

a desire to play billiards about fifteen hundred years before the game is first recorded. As essayist Bill Bryson writes, "Whether by design or ignorance, [Shakespeare] could be breathtakingly casual with the facts when it suited his purposes to do so."[18]

While rewriting history to suit his purposes, Shakespeare was also frequently casual about language, sometimes composing jumbled lines that have defied interpretation. The most famous and confusing Shakespearian line is from *King Lear:* "Swithald footed thrice the old a nellthu night more and her nine fold bid her, O light and her troth plight and arint thee, with arint thee."[19]

That line continues to baffle literary scholars four hundred years after it was written. Shakespeare also invented dozens of words and terms that have become permanent additions to the English language. Some of the Shakespearian phrases that remain in use today include "good riddance," "heart of gold," "wear your heart on your sleeve," "in a pickle," "vanish into thin air," "makes your hair stand on end," "wild goose chase," "sorry sight," and "a piece of work." Robert Bucholz and Newton Key describe Shakespeare's impact: "No historian, and quite possibly no scholar, can do justice to, let alone explain, the dramatic power, the beauty of language, or the insight into the human condition demonstrated by the plays of William Shakespeare."[20]

Controversial Works

Historians estimate that between 1585 and 1613, Shakespeare composed about 154 sonnets, 2 long narrative poems, and 150 plays—38 of which survive. While he is remembered for his poetic influence on the English language, during his life Shakespeare was known for expressing political views that could have led to a prison sentence or worse. However, the playwright avoided royal wrath by voicing antigovernment sentiments using a set of secret code words. According to author Clare Asquith, Shakespeare was a devout Catholic who condemned what he viewed as a repressive Protestant regime:

> [Shakespeare] adopted some of the more general Catholic code terms that were current, such as the use of the words "tempest"

or "storm" to signify England's troubles. . . . Constancy in love was Shakespeare's way of alluding to the importance of a true faith in the "old religion." More specifically, his puns and metaphors often circled around certain key phrases. For instance, to be "sunburned" or "tanned," as are his heroines Viola, Imogen and Portia, was to be close to God and so understood as a true Catholic.[21]

The Elizabethan playwright Ben Jonson was not as subtle as Shakespeare. Jonson, who began his career in the late 1590s, wrote satirical plays that generated widespread controversy. Jonson was even arrested and jailed for sedition after authorities accused him of mocking Queen Elizabeth in his 1597 play *The Isle of Dogs*.

Plagues and Plays

The controversial works by Jonson and others attracted the venomous wrath of religious leaders and government officials, who found little to love about plays, playwrights, and theaters. Actors were compared to vagabonds, thieves, and cheaters, and their work was likened to begging. Plays were called indecent and morally corrupting. As late as 1565, presentation of plays was forbidden in London taverns, inns, or restaurants. Ten years later, the vice mayor of Cambridge warned against profit-making producers, or "light and decayed persons, who for filthy lucre are mynded . . . [to] sett up in open places shewes of unlawfull, hurtfull, pernicious and unhonest [nature]."[22]

Some even blamed the Black Death on the immorality of the theater. As the minister T. White told the congregation at St. Paul's Cathedral in 1577: "The cause of the plagues is sinne [sin], if you looke to it well; and the cause of sinne are playes; therefore the cause of plagues are playes."[23]

Rowdy Stinkards

Whatever the thoughts of aristocrats and religious leaders, Elizabethans from all walks of life crowded into playhouses. Audiences might include gallant gentleman and noble ladies. Aristocrats mixed with pickpockets, prostitutes, scholars, and merchants. Playhouses were also popular with middle-class housewives who had the time and money to attend plays in the afternoon. Women might attend in groups of six to eight, accompanied by a footman, a male servant who drove the women to

The illustrious playwright William Shakespeare wrote hundreds of sonnets and plays. He was as deft with comedy as with tragedy and history.

the theater, purchased the tickets, and acted as a guardian to fend off unwanted advances from rowdy men.

While private playhouses were known for their comfortable seats, the yards of amphitheaters were notoriously foul and uncomfortable. They were often overbooked, with hundreds of customers who smoked tobacco, drank beer and wine, ate raw onions, and never bathed or washed their clothes. In 1606 Thomas Dekker described the audience at the Blackfriars Theatre as "Stinkards, who were so glewed [glued] together in crowdes with their Steames of strong breath, that when they came forth, their faces lookt as if they had beene parboiled."[24]

Unlike polite theatergoers in modern times, Elizabethans were loud and opinionated. During an average performance spectators shouted, hissed, laughed, stamped their feet, and clapped continually. A poor performance might lead audience members to stand on their seats, shout curses, spit, and throw tankards of ale and rotten vegetables at the actors. On a few occasions, when plays mocked the follies of aristocrats and gave voice to social resentments, rowdy audiences were transformed into riotous mobs.

"All Good Sciences"

While the English Renaissance is remembered mainly for its literary achievements, it was also an era of scientific advancement. Elizabeth was intensely focused on transforming England into a world power through the use of science and technology. As the queen wrote around 1575, she was interested in promoting "all good sciences and wise and learned inventions tending to the benefit of the commonwealth of our said Realms and Dimensions, and serving for the defense thereof."[25] To this end, Elizabeth directed large sums of money toward research in mining, metallurgy, navigation, and weapons technology. William Cecil, the queen's secretary of state and lord treasurer, was in charge of funding new inventions, which included a knitting machine, the thermometer, and improved battering rams and armor. Some of the most appreciated Elizabethan inventions were undoubtedly frozen chicken, bottled beer, and the flush toilet.

Ben Jonson's *Humours*

Ben Jonson was one of the most renowned playwrights of the Elizabethan era. Born in 1572, Jonson began his career writing plays called humours. These comedies involved eccentric characters, each of whom represented a different temperament, or humour, such as optimism, ambition, anger, laziness, or gloominess. Jonson's humours included *Every Man in His Humour* (1597), *Every Man out of His Humour* (1598), and *Humour* (1599).

Jonson's own personal humours included a short temper and a large ego. During the early 1600s, these traits gave rise to what was known as the War of the Theatres. In the competitive world of Elizabethan theater, Jonson began the war with his play *The Poetaster*. This piece mercilessly mocked Thomas Dekker and John Marston, two popular playwrights of the era. In 1601 Dekker and Marston responded by writing *Satiromastix*, which portrayed Jonson as a vain fool.

Beyond offending other playwrights with his words, Jonson often irritated powerful authorities. His arrest record was almost as long as his list of plays. Jonson was briefly jailed and tortured for satirizing Elizabeth I's courtiers in 1597. He was charged with treason in 1603 for writing *Sejanus, His Fall*, a play that questioned the powers of royal authorities, using Roman history as a context. Jonson was arrested several more times for his plays and once for killing a man in a duel. Somehow he avoided long prison sentences and died at age sixty-five in 1637.

Another government official, Francis Bacon, who served as lord chancellor of England, was a renowned Renaissance philosopher and scientist. Bacon developed the scientific method for conducting research. Bacon's method is based on performing a repetitive cycle of experiments, forming scientific theories, and having independent scientists verify the results. Bacon wrote several books, including *The New Method*, which were extremely influential in later centuries.

Advances in scientific method, the evolution of theater, and other aspects of the Renaissance were made possible by the growth in literacy. By the early seventeenth century, nearly everyone from Queen Elizabeth to the average London merchant could appreciate and understand the eloquent expressions of Elizabethan thinkers. The words of these scientists, poets, historians, and playwrights resonated for centuries and helped make the Renaissance one of the most important cultural events in English history.

Chapter 4

Privateers, Explorers, and the Pirate Queen

In the southernmost part of England, a large peninsula known as West Country juts out into the ocean. To the south and east lie the English Channel and the European continent. To the west is the vast Atlantic Ocean. During the Elizabethan era, the West Country town of Plymouth, 190 miles (306km) southwest of London, was a bustling port. Traders, explorers, diplomats, and travelers launched their voyages from the Plymouth Sound.

With its strategic location as the jumping-off point for world voyages, the Plymouth region was also home to some of England's most prominent privateers and explorers, men who were known as the sea dogs. John Hawkins was a second-generation seafarer whose wealthy father commanded a fleet of merchant ships out of Plymouth during the reign of Henry VIII. Hawkins's cousin, the famed privateer Francis Drake, grew up in Devon county, where Plymouth is located.

With its port, shipyard, and repair facilities, Plymouth was also home to a fleet of 64 English warships in the mid-1500s. When the Spanish Armada—with over 130 ships, 25,000 sailors and soldiers, and 2,500 cannons—attempted to invade England in 1588, the first actions took place off the Plymouth coast.

Religion, Trade, and Politics

The battle between the English navy and the powerful Spanish Armada was a culmination of a global feud that began in 1562, only four years into the reign of Queen Elizabeth I. Like many wars over the centuries, the disputes were centered on religion and trade. The religious conflict centered on Spanish king Philip II, who was seen throughout Europe as the defender of the Catholic faith. During the 1560s there was a constant fear among Elizabethans that Spain was about to invade Protestant England and return the nation to Catholicism.

The conflict over trade also involved the Spanish, who at the time had near-total control of the seas. When Elizabeth was crowned, England had no colonies in the New World, and the powerful Spanish navy aggressively prevented the English from trading on the Spanish Main. With a relatively weak Royal Navy, Elizabeth believed that the only way England could establish a presence in the New World—while reaping its limitless riches—was through piracy.

In previous decades the pirate trade had been dominated by smugglers and cutthroats. When Elizabeth endorsed privateering, sea plundering became increasingly identified with both patriotic motives and the struggle to maintain Protestantism. In the years that followed, Elizabethan foreign policy was written by English privateers, who manned between one hundred and two hundred pirate ships that plied the waters of Africa, the Caribbean, and the Americas. Some of the most famous pirates, like Hawkins and Drake, were granted knighthoods and celebrated as national heroes for succeeding against the odds.

Slave Trading

The first conflict between Spain and England in the New World was instigated by Hawkins. In 1563 the sea dog went into the slave-trading business with a royal permit issued by Elizabeth. Capturing slaves in Africa, selling them in the Caribbean, and shipping sugar and rum back to Europe made for a highly profitable business. Hawkins was an experienced English trader, and there is little doubt he viewed his slave-trading permit as royal permission to harass Spanish business interests while getting rich. With financial backing from the treasurer of the Royal Navy and several wealthy London traders, Hawkins set sail for Africa with three ships manned by a seasoned crew that included his cousin Francis Drake.

In early 1563 Hawkins sailed 2,000 miles (3218km) down the coast of Africa and gathered about four hundred slaves over the course of four months. On the long journey through rough seas to the Caribbean, the slaves were fed a meager diet of beans and water. About half died during the journey. When Hawkins arrived in present-day Puerto Rico and the Dominican Republic, he had a ready market for those who survived. He traded the slaves for dozens of chests filled with pearls, gold, and silver, fifteen hundred barrels of sugar, and an equal number of animal hides. The riches were so great that Hawkins had to charter two Spanish ships to help him carry his profits.

Hawkins returned home safely. He had a private meeting with Elizabeth in August 1563 and gave the queen a portion of his profits. In return Elizabeth provided Hawkins with a massive carrack, the 700-ton (635–metric ton) *Jesus of Lubeck*, for his next mission.

The First Battle in a Long War

Hawkins engaged in several more slaving missions to the New World. He survived leaky ships, hurricanes, and disease while selling slaves, plundering foreign ships, and burning and looting small villages. After wreaking havoc up and down the eastern coast of Mexico, Hawkins had a disastrous confrontation with Spanish forces at San Juan de Ulúa in what is now Veracruz, Mexico. This represented the first battle in what would become an ongoing conflict between the two dominant sea powers, England and Spain.

On September 23, 1568, the English fleet of five ships, including one under the command of Drake, was attacked by Spanish commander Francisco Luján. A full-scale battle ensued, cannons were fired repeatedly, and the *Jesus of Lubeck* sank in the bay. Hawkins escaped, but five hundred of his men were killed. The English also lost a year's worth of loot valued at millions of pounds.

Although the Battle of San Juan de Ulúa was between two small fleets of ships in a distant land, it made one point clear. If the English wanted to establish a presence in the New World, they would have to fight the Spanish for that right. And while the final showdown between England and Spain would not erupt for another twenty years, the two nations remained on war footing after the Battle of San Juan de Ulúa.

The Dragon and the Pirate Queen

Like his cousin, Drake had a strong relationship with Elizabeth. The queen viewed the dashing young privateer as a man of action who could be relied upon to carry out difficult orders. As the Spanish diplomat Bernardino de Mendoza noted: "The Queen shows extraordinary favor to Drake and never fails to speak to him when she goes out in public, conversing with him for a long time."[26]

Drake first gained the queen's attention in the early 1570s for a series of daring raids in and around the town of Nombre de Dios on the Atlantic side of the Panama isthmus. Nombre de Dios, which was about the size of Plymouth, was the major shipping port used by the Spanish treasure fleet. Silver, gold, and precious gems from South America were brought to the town and stored in crude warehouses. Little wonder that Drake called Nombre de Dios "the treasure house of the world."[27]

Twice a year a flotilla of Spanish galleons picked up the wealth in Nombre de Dios and shipped it to Seville. Without the shipments of gold and silver, King Philip II would have been unable to keep Spain from bankruptcy.

Drake and his small crew arrived in the Nombre de Dios region in February 1571 and befriended escaped black slaves called *cimarrones* who lived in the area. The cimarrones hated the Spanish rulers and provided Drake with important inside information. They told Drake that Nombre de Dios was not fortified and there was no garrison nearby to protect it.

Drake plied the waters of the Spanish Main around Nombre de Dios for three months but did not invade the town. During this period his crew intercepted twelve Spanish vessels and seized extremely valuable gold, silver, and other goods. After this mission, the Spanish began calling Drake *El Draque*, or "The Dragon."

Queen Elizabeth knights Sir Francis Drake on the deck of his ship, the
Golden Hind. *Drake received his knighthood from a grateful queen*
after he returned from the New World with a fortune in gold, silver,
and other items taken from a captured Spanish ship.

Drake returned to England without ever landing in Nombre de Dios
and gave a share of his booty to Elizabeth. However, the exploits of the
privateers would have been scandalous if linked to the queen or her advisors. To avoid any appearance of approval, Elizabeth secretly encouraged
the privateers while publicly distancing herself from their actions. While
this might have worked at home, the queen's support for privateering
was well known to Philip. In the royal courts of Spain, Elizabeth was
referred to as the "pirate queen." As the years passed, Philip became convinced that the only way to stop the depredations of the swashbuckling
sea dogs was to invade England.

Stealing Funds for a Royal Navy

The pirate queen had many advisors, and one of them, John Dee, had spies in Spain. Dee knew that Philip was using his gold to increase the size of the Spanish Armada with the aim of conquering England. In 1576 Dee presented a paper to the queen with a thirteen-point plan for building a navy powerful enough to resist Spain's fighting forces. Dee envisioned a Royal Navy consisting of seventy-seven tall ships manned by 6,660 well-paid sailors who would patrol England's coasts and protect the nation from enemy invasion. Elizabeth wanted to carry out Dee's plan but needed a great fortune to build such a navy. The queen commissioned Drake to sail to South America and steal the necessary funds from the Spanish.

On December 13, 1577, Drake sailed out of Plymouth Sound standing at the wheel of the galleon he later named the *Golden Hind*. He had five other ships under his command. Drake's crew of 164 men was heading to present-day Chile on the west coast of South America. Although it is unknown whether Drake planned to do more than attack Spanish galleons filled with Peruvian gold, his mission led him to sail around the world, making him the first Englishman to circumnavigate the earth.

Drake's fleet arrived on the eastern coast of South America on April 5, 1578. By this time several ships had been lost in storms, reducing the fleet to three vessels. The remaining ships sailed south and reached the Strait of Magellan at the southernmost point of South America in September. The Strait of Magellan is a notoriously rough body of water where the Atlantic and Pacific Oceans meet. When the English ships entered the strait, they ran into high seas and ferocious storms. One ship sank, and another turned back to England. Drake described the conditions in his journal: "[We are] worn out by so many and so long intolerable toils; the like whereof, it is supposed, no traveler hath felt, neither hath there ever been such a tempest, so violent and of such continuance since Noah's flood."[28]

The *Golden Hind* was now the last ship sailing, but despite his reduced circumstances, Drake did not lose sight of his mission. On

March 1, 1579, Drake captured the heavily armed Spanish treasure ship *Cacafuego*. He described looting the ship: "We found in her some fruits, sugars, meal and other victuals [food], and . . . a certain quantity of jewels, precious stones, 13 chest of ryals of plate [silver coins], 80 pound weight in gold, 26 tons of uncoined silver, two very fair guilt silver drinking bottles, and the like trifles, valued at 360,000 pesos."[29]

The treasure taken from the *Cacafuego* was the richest prize ever captured by any pirate or privateer. News of the heist quickly reached top Spanish commanders in the region. While dozens of Spain's finest warships began an intense search for the *Golden Hind*, Drake headed northwest into the unknown.

In June 1579 Drake reached present-day San Diego, California. He called the land Nova Albion, Latin for "New Britain." The crew continued up the California coast before heading west once again. On September 26, 1580, the *Golden Hind* finally made it back to Plymouth after two years and nine months at sea. Of his original crew, only fifty-nine survived, but the treasures made them all wealthy men. Seven months after his return, Drake received a knighthood from the queen.

Singeing the King's Beard

By the time Drake returned to England, Hawkins was the treasurer of the Royal Navy. In this role Hawkins used a portion of Drake's pillaged Spanish gold to build a new, more advanced warship. The revolutionary galleons were "race-built," that is, cut down in size to be fast and maneuverable. They were sleek, long, and described by Hawkins as "low and snug"[30] in the water. Although ships with sails cannot navigate directly into the wind, the English galleons had masts designed to sail as directly into the wind as possible. As British historian Winston Graham explains, "Such ships could sail nearer the wind and were more maneuverable than any warships that had been built before."[31]

As the English navy grew in strength, religious conflicts continued to fester. Philip II in Spain and the pope in Rome were both committed to returning Catholicism to England. In 1585 Pope Sixtus V issued an edict promising Spain an enormous sum to destroy what he called

Religious Motives of Sailors

British historian Ian Friel describes how religious beliefs affected the actions of Elizabethan sailors:

> Religion was a constant presence at sea, with services held once or twice a day aboard most ships. . . . Given the brutal religious conflicts of the period, sailors were able to claim the highest motives for theft, destruction and violence. This was certainly apparent with some of [navigator] Edward Fenton's men during his 1582 expedition to Africa and South America. They declared that they were "bound in duty to spoil all papists [Catholics], as enemies to God & our sovereign, of what country so ever they were."

Ian Friel, "Guns, Gales & God: Elizabeth I's 'Merchant Navy,'" *History Today*, January 2010. www.historytoday.com.

the heretical state of England. Philip accepted the offer and raised even more money for the effort he called the Enterprise of England.

By early 1587 the Spanish port of Cádiz was busy as warships of the Spanish Armada gathered and sailors trained for an all-out assault on England. While Philip's enterprise was meant to be a secret, Elizabeth's spies had learned of the mission. On April 12 the queen unleashed Drake to stop the invasion before it started. Eighteen days later Drake arrived off the coast of Cádiz. When the seven English warships boldly sailed into the harbor in Cádiz firing their cannons, panic overwhelmed the Spanish sailors and they abandoned their posts. Drake's crewmen boarded the abandoned vessels of the Spanish Armada, looted them, and burned them to the waterline. Of the sixty or so naval and merchant vessels in Cádiz, thirty-seven were destroyed by Drake.

The attack nearly destroyed the Armada and caused great damage to Philip's finances. When Drake returned to England victorious, he told the queen he had "singed the king's beard."[32] However, Philip was still determined to invade England. He borrowed money and rebuilt the Armada. Within a year, the Spanish fleet had grown to over one hundred fifty vessels. It included warships, troop transports, and provision ships. Although the Royal Navy consisted of two hundred ships, the British were short on arms and supplies.

The Crusade Against England

The queen did not believe the Royal Navy was ready to withstand the Armada, and in early July 1588 English diplomats were frantically negotiating with Spanish and papal representatives to hold off an attack. Negotiations broke down, however, and the Spanish fleet appeared off the coast of the West Country on July 19. The ships of the Armada were packed with seven thousand sailors and seventeen thousand heavily armed soldiers. However, the Spanish commander, Alonso Pérez de Guzmán, had little experience at sea. Philip picked him to lead the invasion because of his noble lineage. This proved to be a major mistake. Guzmán ordered the Spanish Armada to sail with its ships in a crescent formation with warships on the outside. These large ships protected the slow-moving troop and provision vessels inside the crescent. This put the Armada at a strategic disadvantage. The formation limited the ability of the warships to move quickly and independently if necessary. In addition, the Spanish did not have long-range cannons capable of sinking English ships from a distance.

Guzmán planned for the Armada to sail directly up to the ships of the Royal Navy. Spanish soldiers would board the English ships with overwhelming force and kill the sailors. There was one major problem with this scheme. The English warships designed by Hawkins were fast and agile. They could tack close to the Spanish ships for intense combat or stand at a distance of around 300 yards (274m) and pound them with cannon fire.

Philip was warned of the strategic problems the Armada might encounter, but he ignored his advisors. According to Robert Bucholz and

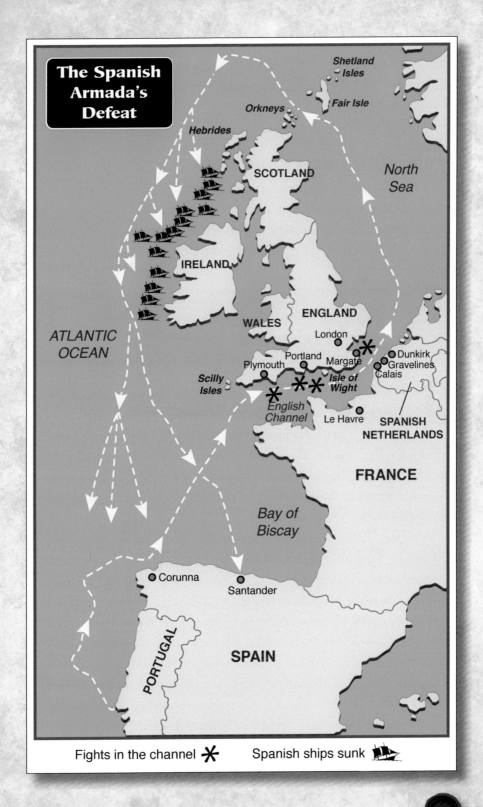

The Spanish Armada's Defeat

Shetland Isles
Fair Isle
Orkneys
Hebrides
SCOTLAND
North Sea
IRELAND
ATLANTIC OCEAN
WALES
ENGLAND
London
Scilly Isles
Plymouth
Portland
Margate
Isle of Wight
English Channel
Dunkirk
Gravelines
Calais
Le Havre
SPANISH NETHERLANDS
FRANCE
Bay of Biscay
Corunna
Santander
PORTUGAL
SPAIN

Fights in the channel ✱   Spanish ships sunk

Newton Key, as a "person of deep Catholic faith the king was certain that God would favor the Armada as a means to punish England for their Protestant heresy. . . . Philip and his Spanish subjects could not conceive that this crusade could fail."[33]

Scattering the Armada

There is little doubt that the English also believed God was on their side. But they had also built a tough, maneuverable fleet with ships bearing names like *Revenge* and *Victory*, meant to shake the enemy's confidence. And the English understood that defeat was not an option.

Frobisher's Gold Fever

In May 1577 Elizabeth I and some of the richest aristocrats in England were pooling millions of pounds to fund privateer and explorer Martin Frobisher's expedition to present-day Newfoundland, Canada. The Elizabethan aristocrats had a bad case of gold fever. They believed rumors that Canada was filled with untold riches in the form of gold ore, which could be mined and shipped back to England.

Upon their arrival in present-day Nunavut in northern Canada, Frobisher and his crew began digging up black rocks believed to contain gold ore. As the summer drew to a close, Frobisher filled his ships with almost 200 tons (181 metric tons) of shiny rocks. Upon returning to England Frobisher was treated to a hero's welcome. Meanwhile, his rocks were analyzed for gold content. After months of rigorous study, it was determined that the metallic, gold-like substance in the black rock was worthless iron pyrite, also known as fool's gold. Frobisher's investors lost millions. In later years Frobisher launched several more unsuccessful expeditions to Canada in search of gold.

The Royal Navy was not only England's first line of defense, it was the only line of defense. If the Armada prevailed, the English had no real standing army to fight battle-hardened Spanish soldiers. If the Armada achieved landfall, the English would have to rely on two hundred thousand untrained civilians armed with their own muskets, axes, and pitchforks. As the Armada threatened, Elizabeth traveled to Tilbury on the eastern coast of England to rally her civilian army:

I know I have the body but of a weak and feeble woman; but I have the heart and stomach of a king, and of a king of England, too—and take foul scorn that . . . any prince of Europe, should dare to invade the borders of my realm. To which rather than any dishonor shall grow by me, I myself will take up arms, I myself will be your general, judge, and rewarder of every one of your virtues in the field.[34]

While the English farmers, fishers, and tradespeople stood ready to die for their queen, the battle between the Armada and Royal Navy unfolded over the course of several weeks. During the Elizabethan era, navies were dependent on tides, winds, and weather. Although the Armada first appeared on July 19, the decisive battle did not occur until the July 28 near Calais, France, on the south side of the English Channel.

As the Armada sat anchored, the English sailed upwind and sent eight fireships into the tightly packed crescent formation. Fireships, known as hellburners, are large, unmanned warships filled with gunpowder and extremely flammable materials such as tar, pitch (plant resin), and brimstone (sulfur). As the fireships sailed toward the Armada, the fleet cut its anchor cables and scattered. Only a few Spanish ships actually burned, but those that fled ran into the cannons of the Royal Navy. The ships of the Armada were sunk one by one, and the Spanish invasion was thwarted. Those that remained afloat sailed north around Scotland but ran into heavy storms and violent gales. The English referred to these storms as the Protestant Wind.

English fire ships, loaded with flammables and set ablaze, explode in the midst of the Spanish Armada. Though few Spanish ships actually burned, those that fled were sunk by the cannons of the Royal Navy.

While exact figures are hard to come by, it is estimated that Spain lost five thousand to fifteen thousand men and half its ships. Meanwhile, Elizabeth I had survived her greatest challenge. To celebrate, she minted commemorative metals that said "God blew and they were scattered."[35] While the troubles with Spain and other Catholic nations would continue for decades, Elizabethan England was richer and stronger, thanks to the bravery, intelligence, and cunning of admirals in the Royal Navy.

Chapter 5

What Is the Legacy of Elizabethan England?

When Queen Elizabeth I died on March 24, 1603, at age sixty-nine, a court diarist reported her death: "This morning, about three o'clock, Her Majesty departed this life, mildly like a lamb, easily like a ripe apple from a tree, with a slight shiver, without a groan. . . . I doubt not but she is amongst the royal saints in Heaven in eternal joys."[36] With this final royal shiver, the Tudor dynasty, which began in 1485, came to an end.

Under Elizabeth, important aspects of English society were transformed. England was largely united in matters of culture, religion, and economics. English naval power was growing, and exploration in the New World was accelerating. Commerce and trade improved the fortunes of the growing middle class, and the nation experienced a renaissance in the arts and science.

Despite these changes, the queen's subjects had no great love for her at the time of her death. She left behind a nation deeply in debt due to expenses incurred while fighting the Spanish. Aristocrats complained persistently about paying high taxes for the Poor Laws. Almost everyone else in Elizabethan England was struggling to survive. People were battered by unemployment, petty crime, overcrowded slums, and periodic food shortages. Catholics had been persecuted for years, and small groups continued to plot against Protestant rule. Thus, the news of Elizabeth's death was cause for celebration among her former subjects. People danced in the streets and held drunken parties around bonfires. And with the announcement that James I, king of Scotland and a member of the House of Stuart, was to be her successor, the celebrants cheered, "We have a king!"[37]

The Anglican Communion

Despite the nation's problems at the end of the Elizabeth's reign, the queen's policies had a lasting impact on life in England and elsewhere. Perhaps the most important legacy of Elizabeth's reign is that she prevented a religious civil war in England, despite coming to power at a time when such a war seemed imminent. While there were periods of persecution against Catholics during her reign, Elizabeth managed to quell religious rebellion by instructing the Anglican Communion to follow a policy known in Latin as *via media*, or the middle path. The church defined this as following the middle path between what it saw as the extremes of Protestantism and Catholicism. As Chaplain Dwight Longenecker explains: "Anglicans were meant to be open to the truths to which both Protestants and Catholics witnessed. In matters of liturgy, sacred music, spirituality, and doctrine, the Anglican was meant to be informed by both the Catholic and the Reformed [Protestant] traditions."[38]

By the time of Elizabeth's death, Anglicanism was establishing itself in the New World. The first Anglican church in North America was founded in Jamestown in the Colony of Virginia in 1607. As Anglicanism took hold in the American colonies in the following decades, each church was free to institute varying degrees of Catholic and Protestant traditions, depending on the makeup of the congregation. When the British Empire expanded in the late 1700s to include India, Australia, and parts of Africa, the Middle East, and Pacific regions, Anglican missionaries continued to follow the middle path guided by the traditions found in the Book of Common Prayer.

As Anglican missionaries traveled the world over the centuries, they carried with them the King James Bible. This version of the Old and

The English Tradesmen

The growth of the middle class during Elizabethan times helped propel England into its role as a world power by the eighteenth century. Middle-class people worked as merchants, traders, manufacturers, and artisans. They were bakers, brewers, tailors, glassblowers, and leatherworkers. The rising prosperity of the middle class during the Elizabethan era solidified the power of the British Empire in later centuries. Renaissance scholar Louis B. Wright explains:

> [The] Elizabethan tradesman, the average citizen, was the backbone of progressive enterprise in England and the direct ancestor of a civilization soon to predominate on both sides of the Atlantic. His vigor and strength enabled England to take its place in the front rank of nations. In furtherance of his social ambitions, the Elizabethan business man evolved in a philosophy of success, which emphasized thrift, honesty, industry, and godliness. . . . Substantial commoners, gathering in strength in the sixteenth century, grew in intelligence and mental stature to become the power that was to conquer a new continent [North America] and make England great.

Louis B. Wright, *Middle-Class Culture in Elizabethan England*. Ithaca, NY: Cornell University Press, 1958, p. 1.

New Testaments was written by Elizabethan-era scholars who were appointed to the task by King James I in January 1604, less than one year into his reign. Today the King James Bible holds the record as the most published book in the history of the world. It is the only book with more than 1 billion copies in print.

In the more than four and a half centuries since Parliament enacted the Elizabethan Religious Settlement, Anglicanism has grown to become the third-largest Christian denomination in the world, with 85 million followers in 2011. The Church of England remains one of the most respected institutions in Great Britain. This legacy can be traced to religious reforms instituted under Elizabeth I and the religious scholars who lived during her reign.

The Haves and Have-Nots

Another lasting impact of the Elizabethan era concerns the change in public attitudes toward the poor. The first in a series of Poor Laws was enacted in England in 1563, and they were updated in 1572, 1598, and 1601. Although the acts did not eradicate poverty in England, the Poor Laws were the first government programs in Europe to address poverty. As Robert Bucholz and Newton Key write:

> [The] recognition that the nation as a whole had a responsibility to care for its least fortunate members . . . was remarkably advanced for the time, far ahead of anything on the continent. . . . [The Poor Law] probably did help to tide people over during a crisis. Its existence may even help to explain why, despite real famine in the 1590s and 1620s, England did not experience widespread popular rebellion as did, say, France during the same period. This appearance of paternalism, neighborliness, fairness, and generosity by the haves in English society may have alleviated the misery, or at least forestalled the questioning, of the have-nots.[39]

The Elizabethan Poor Laws formed the basis for England's welfare system well into the nineteenth century. The laws might have been well intentioned, but the system of workhouses and orphanages established by the Poor Laws were cruel and corrupt. By the 1820s the unemployed were required to move into workhouses if they wanted government help. Even at that time, this arrangement was called the "1601 system." This referred to the Poor Relief Act of 1601, which ordered each parish to build poorhouses for the indigent, workhouses for the able-bodied poor, and debtors' prisons for those who were bankrupt.

Conditions inside the 1601 system were deliberately harsh. Men, women, and children were forced to wear uniforms and perform unpleasant jobs such as breaking rocks. Children were effectively treated as slaves, forced into dangerous and deadly work in factories and mines. Those who supervised the workhouses, called matrons and masters, were frequently cruel and abusive and often denied food to inmates. Reformers who protested conditions in the workhouses called them prisons for the poor.

The Legacy of Workhouses

One of the most famous writers in England witnessed the brutality of the 1601 system firsthand. In 1824 the father of Charles Dickens was sent to a debtor's prison. Dickens, then twelve years old, was forced to work in a blacking factory, where shoe polish was made. The ten-hour workdays were grueling, the bosses cruel, and conditions in the rat-infested factory hazardous.

Although Dickens worked in the blacking factory for less than a year, he never forgot the experience. He went on to become one of the most respected authors in history, with a command of the English language seen as second only to Shakespeare. Several of his best-selling books vividly describe the misfortunes of the poor. In the 1837 novel *Oliver Twist*, Dickens tells the story of a boy who was born in a workhouse, starved in an orphanage, and sent to work in a factory when he was nine. In the 1839 novel *David Copperfield*, the lead character spends some time in a workhouse.

Dickens's fiction gave voice to the problems and frustrations of London's lower classes. Although his books were written more than 230 years after the Elizabethan era ended, the lives of the poor were

The legacy of Elizabethan-era Poor Laws can be seen in the writings of Charles Dickens. The laws, though well-intentioned, created a harsh system of workhouses, orphanages, and debtors' prisons. An illustration from Dickens's Oliver Twist *depicts the hungry orphan, Oliver, inside a den of child thieves.*

still governed by Elizabeth's 1601 system. After Dickens shed light on the evils produced by the Poor Laws, reformers gradually instituted a series of improvements to the welfare system first implemented by the Elizabethans.

Ties to India

While Dickens often wrote of London's poor, the city that formed the backdrop for his writing was actually the richest and most spectacular in the world by the nineteenth century. One of the major sources of London's wealth was international trade. And this, too, had roots in the Elizabethan era.

In 1600 Elizabeth granted the East India Company (EIC) a royal charter, an official license to operate a business. The EIC was one of the earliest joint-stock companies, an Elizabethan-era concept resembling modern corporations. The company was formed by two hundred fourteen of England's richest and most influential men, called stockholders, who pooled their money to engage in business transactions.

In 1601 the EIC sent its first fleet of merchant ships to India and Southeast Asia. Within a few years the company had become a successful operation. It established a lucrative international trade in cotton, silk, salt, tea, opium, and saltpeter (potassium nitrate used to make gunpowder). By 1650 the EIC had constructed over twenty factories in India to process and produce trade goods. Seventy years later, more than 15 percent of all English imports were handled by the EIC.

The EIC was able to extend its influence because India was not a united country at this time. The company operated by signing treaties and making alliances with various local princes, who swore their loyalty to England. This allowed the EIC to become a major governing power in India by 1740. It minted money, controlled important administrative offices, and established its own private army overseen by British officers.

In 1757 the EIC took complete control of India, establishing what is called company rule. For the next eighty-five years, British governors who worked for the EIC ran the country. After an Indian rebellion in 1857, the British government took over India and established what is known as the Raj. In the decades that followed, the British Raj built railroads, factories, hospitals, and other infrastructure in India. The poor were repressed, while upper-class Indians were educated in English schools, served in the British military, and worked as government officials. With about twenty thousand British officials and soldiers, the Raj ruled 300 million Indians until the nation gained independence in 1947.

The British Raj has long been controversial. As the British National Archives explains: "Admirers of British rule point to the economic developments, the legal and administrative system, the fact that India became the center of world politics. Critics of British rule generally point out that all of these benefits went to a tiny British ruling class and the majority of Indians gained little."[40]

The Elizabethans and Tobacco

Even as the EIC was taking control of India, a pair of joint-stock companies, the Virginia Company of London and the Virginia Company of Plymouth, were seeking to build new settlements in North America. In 1607 the Virginia Company sent Captain John Smith to establish the Jamestown settlement in Virginia. (Virginia's name was inspired by Elizabeth I's status as the Virgin Queen.)

Smith's group of one hundred forty-four men and boys were ill-prepared for the work of survival in the American wilderness. Many of the settlers were city-bred gentlemen who could not handle a musket, fishing rod, or plow. They unwisely built their fort on a mosquito-infested swamp, far from wild game and good sources of fresh water. The result was widespread hunger and illnesses caused by drinking the brackish water. During the winter of 1609–1610, known as the Starving Time, about a quarter of Jamestown's residents perished.

Unlike the EIC, the Virginia Company did not initially make its investors rich. There was little the settlers could do to make money, and in fact, they struggled just to survive. Conditions changed in 1612, when John Rolf harvested Virginia's first successful tobacco crop. Within two years the stockholders in the Virginia Company were turning a profit selling Virginia tobacco in England.

Explorer Walter Raleigh had first introduced Brazilian-grown tobacco to Elizabeth in 1600. While others smoked tobacco in cigars, Raleigh implored the queen to smoke a pipe. English physicians realized

Impact of the King James Bible

Months after Elizabeth I died, Parliament authorized the creation of the King James Bible. It was produced over the course of seven years by forty-seven religious scholars schooled during the Elizabethan era. Written in flowery prose, the King James Bible contributed even more unique phrases to the English language than did Shakespeare. Over two hundred fifty turns of expression are found in the King James Bible, including, "broken heart," "a cross to bear," "old as the hills," "feet of clay," "bite the dust," "by the skin of your teeth," and "eat, drink, and be merry."

The King James Bible has long been revered for its beauty of language and its faithfulness to ancient Greek- and Hebrew-language versions. In 1881 fifty scholars analyzing the King James Bible wrote: "We have had to study this great Version carefully and minutely, line by line; and the longer we have been engaged upon it the more we have learned to admire its simplicity, its dignity, its power, its happy turns of expression, its general accuracy, and, we must not fail to add, the music of its cadences, and the felicities of its rhythm."

Quoted in *All About Truth*, "King James Bible—Beloved Translation." www.allabouttruth.org.

almost immediately that the substance was unhealthy and addictive, but tobacco was instantly regarded as fashionable. By 1614 tobacco plantations lined the James River in Virginia, and according to English author Barnabe Rich, writing in 1617, "[There] be 7000 shops, in and about London, that doth vent [sell] Tobacco."[41]

The profits from tobacco set off a land rush as settlers flocked to Virginia to make their fortunes in the New World. By 1622 about one thousand English and other European settlers were living in Virginia.

They set up the first government in America, called the House of Burgesses. The land was divided into boroughs and cities, and laws for land ownership were instituted.

The Native Americans in the region, a confederation of tribes known as the Powhatan, were horrified by these developments. While the Powhatan had initially fed the settlers and helped them survive, relations with the newcomers quickly soured. As the English continued to clear more land for tobacco crops, the Powhatan retaliated, hoping to rid their land of foreigners permanently. In what became known as the Indian Massacre of 1622, over three hundred settlers were killed.

While the Powhatan attack was a setback for the settlers, it did not end their occupation of the region. In 1624 James I officially declared Virginia to be a British colony. By the mid-1600s over five thousand settlers lived in the Colony of Virginia, the largest and most successful of the English colonies.

The Puritans in Plymouth

While the Virginia Company of London was reaping tobacco profits, its twin enterprise, the Virginia Company of Plymouth (or the Plymouth Company), was struggling. The Plymouth Company first established the Popham Colony near the present-day town of Phippsburg, Maine, the same year Jamestown was founded. However, most of the settlers did not survive the extreme winter, and those who did abandoned the settlement after one year.

The Plymouth Company remained inactive until 1620, when it granted a settlement charter to the Puritans, a sect of English Protestants. The Puritans formed in 1559 as a reaction to the Elizabethan Religious Settlement. The denomination was controversial for its refusal to accept the middle path of Anglicism. Puritans believed that the Church of England was ungodly, a product of political struggles and human-made doctrines.

The Puritans were divided amongst themselves. Some believed the Church of England needed to be reformed and made more conservative. Other Puritans, called Pilgrims, were separatists. They believed that true Christians should separate themselves from the Church of England.

During Elizabeth's reign, the Pilgrims had been tolerated by the English government. However, James was fearful of their zealotry and considered jailing members of the sect. Fearing persecution, about one hundred fifty Pilgrims fled England to Netherlands in 1608. The Pilgrims were unhappy there, and one hundred two of them decided to move to America in 1620. They boarded the *Mayflower* in August and landed near present-day Provincetown, Massachusetts, on November 13.

Like the settlers in Jamestown, the Pilgrims struggled to survive in the North American wilderness. By December, in the midst of the bone-chilling New England winter, the Pilgrims were living on the *Mayflower* as they struggled to build a settlement near present-day Plymouth. Wracked by disease and starvation, forty-five Pilgrims died the first year. The following year, with the help of the indigenous Wampanoag people, the Pilgrims gained a foothold in the New World.

The growth of trade during Elizabeth's reign set in motion a legacy of colonial expansion in the New World and elsewhere. England's hold on some of its New World possessions ended with the colonists' victory in the Revolutionary War. In a copy of the famous painting by Emanuel Leutze, General George Washington and his troops cross the Delaware during the war.

In the years that followed, the Massachusetts Bay Colony expanded as English settlers continued to arrive. By 1643 about two thousand Puritans and Pilgrims lived in Massachusetts, and others established thriving colonies in Connecticut and Rhode Island.

The Thirteen Colonies

By 1700 the British colonies in North American were attracting settlers from Germany, Netherlands, France, and elsewhere. The population was over 270,000, plus about 21,000 African slaves. Other colonies were founded, including New York, New Jersey, North and South Carolina, and New Hampshire. Georgia became the thirteenth colony in 1733.

People in the thirteen colonies were governed by English kings but had much more freedom than people in England. Each colony had a General Assembly, and by 1750 most free men could vote to elect representatives. While the representatives managed local matters, the colonies were under the rule of English kings and Parliament.

The natural resources of the thirteen colonies brought great wealth to England, as did taxes levied on the colonists. However, the colonists were unhappy with English rule. In 1776 the colonies declared independence from England, precipitating the American Revolution. After the revolutionaries defeated the British and signed the treaty ending the war in 1783, the US Constitution was adopted in 1787.

The United States grew into the richest and most powerful country in the world. Over the centuries historians have attributed the success of the country to what is called the Protestant work ethic. This concept of viewing work as a duty that benefits both the individual and society has long been interpreted as an obligation to work hard. The Protestant work ethic is another vestige of the Elizabethan era that continues to guide the lives of millions throughout the world.

The Best of Times and the Worst of Times

Despite the lasting impact of the Elizabethans, the era might best be summed up by the opening line of the 1859 book *A Tale of Two Cities* by Charles Dickens: "It was the best of times, it was the worst of times, it was the age of wisdom, it was the age of foolishness, it was the epoch of belief, it was the epoch of incredulity, it was the season of Light, it was the season of Darkness, it was the spring of hope, it was the winter of despair."[42] Although Dickens was referring to nineteenth-century London, the lines could also describe life during Elizabeth's reign. The Elizabethan era was an exciting age of discovery and a bloody time of piracy and war on the high seas. It was the era of literary geniuses like Shakespeare, Marlowe, and Bacon and a time of epidemics like the Black Plague. The bejeweled Elizabeth ruled as a wise and wealthy monarch while thousands of her subjects starved.

Like many other epochs, the Elizabethan era was undeniably a time of contrasts. But few other eras in modern history have left such lasting impressions on the world. The Elizabethans set up the first corporations and were involved in the founding of the United States. And the English language went on to become the international language of commerce.

The Elizabethan era also remains alive in the modern media. The life of Queen Elizabeth I has provided inspiration for at least four operas, several dozen films and TV shows, countless books, and even a few video games. Shakespeare's works have been adapted to more than four hundred feature-length films and television shows, and his plays and poems remain required reading for students throughout the world. From Great Britain to the Caribbean, India, and the United States, the legacy of the Elizabethans continues to resonate more than four centuries after Elizabeth's death.

Source Notes 🌐

Introduction: The Defining Characteristics of Elizabethan England

1. Quoted in Robert Bucholz and Newton Key, *Early Modern England, 1485–1714*. Malden, MA: Blackwell, 2004, p. 112.
2. Quoted in Royal Museums Greenwich, "The Evolution of Elizabeth's Image," 2012. www.rmg.co.uk.

Chapter One: What Conditions Led to the Elizabethan Era?

3. Louis B. Wright, *Middle-Class Culture in Elizabethan England*. Ithaca, NY: Cornell University Press, 1958, p. 122.
4. Bucholz and Key, *Early Modern England, 1485–1714*, p. 64.
5. Derek Wilson, *A Brief History of Henry VIII*. London: Constable & Robinson, 2009, pp. 183–184.
6. Quoted in Bucholz and Key, *Early Modern England, 1485–1714*, p. 75.

Chapter Two: Rich and Poor in England

7. Quoted in A.N. Wilson, *The Elizabethans*. New York: Farrar, Straus and Giroux, 2011, p. 29.
8. A.N. Wilson, *The Elizabethans*, p. 31.
9. Quoted in Liza Picard, *Elizabeth's London: Everyday Life in Elizabethan London*. New York: St. Martin's, 2003, p. 33.
10. Picard, *Elizabeth's London: Everyday Life in Elizabethan London*, pp. 34–35.
11. Quoted in Picard, *Elizabeth's London: Everyday Life in Elizabethan London*, p. 91.
12. Quoted in F.P. Wilson, *The Plague in Shakespeare's London*. Oxford: Oxford University Press, 1963, pp. 43–44.

13. Quoted in Tudor Place, "The Act of Supremacy," 2012. www.tudor place.com.

14. Quoted in Carol Kazmierczak Manzione, *Christ's Hospital of London, 1552–1598: A Passing Deed of Pity*. Cranbury, NJ: Associated University Presses, 1995, p. 15.

Chapter Three: The Elizabethan Renaissance

15. Quoted in Deborah E. Harkness, *The Jewel House*. New Haven, CT: Yale University Press, 2007, pp. 1–2.

16. Quoted in John Phillips, *The Reformation of Images: Destruction of Art in England, 1535–1660*. Berkeley: University of California Press, 1973, p. 53.

17. Quoted in Deborah H. Cibelli, "Tudor and Elizabethan Painting," Art & Architecture of the British Renaissance, 2008. www.nicholls .edu.

18. Bill Bryson, *Shakespeare: The World as a Stage*. New York: Harper-Collins, 2007, pp. 108–109.

19. Quoted in Robert Darnton, "The Heresies of Bibliography," *New York Review of Books*, May 29, 2003. www.nybooks.com.

20. Bucholz and Key, *Early Modern England, 1485–1714*, p. 197.

21. Quoted in Vanessa Thorpe, "Shakespeare Was a Political Rebel Who Wrote in Code, Claims Author," *Guardian* (London), August 27, 2005. www.guardian.co.uk.

22. Quoted in Gerald Eades Bentley, ed., *The Seventeenth-Century Stage*. Chicago: University of Chicago Press, 1968, p. 58.

23. Quoted in F.P. Wilson, *The Plague in Shakespeare's London*, p. 52.

24. Thomas Dekker, *The Seven Deadly Sins of London*. London: English Scholar's Library, 1879, p. 32.

25. Quoted in Harkness, *The Jewel House*, pp. 163–164.

Chapter Four: Privateers, Explorers, and the Pirate Queen

26. Quoted in Peter Brimacombe, *All the Queen's Men*. New York: St. Martin's, 2000, p. 73.

27. Quoted in Susan Ronald, *The Pirate Queen*. New York: Harper-Collins, 2007, p. 150.

28. Quoted in Ronald, *The Pirate Queen*, p. 221.

29. Francis Drake, *The World Encompassed*. New York: Da Capo, 1969, p. 59.

30. Quoted in Winston Graham, *The Spanish Armada*. London: Collins, 1987, p. 95.

31. Graham, *The Spanish Armada*, p. 97.

32. Quoted in Bucholz and Key, *Early Modern England, 1485–1714*, p. 133.

33. Bucholz and Key, *Early Modern England, 1485–1714*, p. 135.

34. Quoted in Leah S. Marcus, Janel Mueller, and Mary Beth Rose, eds., *Elizabeth I: Collected Works*. Chicago: University of Chicago Press, 2000, p. 326.

35. Quoted in Bucholz and Key, *Early Modern England, 1485–1714*, p. 138.

Chapter Five: What Is the Legacy of Elizabethan England?

36. Quoted in Richard Rex, *The Tudors*. Gloucestershire, UK: Tempus, 2005, p. 269.

37. Quoted in John Morrill, *The Oxford Illustrated History of Tudor and Stuart Britain*. Oxford: Oxford University Press, 1996, p. 346.

38. Dwight Longenecker, "Could Anglican Ordinariates Be the Real 'Anglican Middle Way'?," Catholic Online, March 16, 2010. www.catholic.org.

39. Bucholz and Key, *Early Modern England, 1485–1714*, p. 177.

40. National Archives, "Living in the British Empire," 2012. www.nationalarchives.gov.uk.

41. Quoted in Adolphus William Ward, *The Cambridge History of English Literature*, vol. 5. Cambridge: Cambridge University Press, p. 358.

42. Charles Dickens, *A Tale of Two Cities*. London: Nisbet, 1902, p. 3.

Important People of Elizabethan England

Anne Boleyn: Born in 1502, Anne Boleyn became queen consort after marrying Henry VIII in 1533. The marriage sparked England's split from the Catholic Church and resulted in the birth of Elizabeth I. Anne was falsely convicted of adultery, incest, and treason and was beheaded at Henry's behest in 1536.

James Burbage: Burbage was the leading promoter of plays during the Shakespearian era. He built the first independent playhouse in England, The Theatre, in 1576.

Catherine of Aragon: Born in 1485, Catherine of Aragon was the daughter of King Ferdinand and Queen Isabella of Spain. Catherine married Henry VIII and gave birth to Mary Tudor (Queen Mary I).

Thomas Cromwell: Cromwell was the 1st Earl of Essex and became chief advisor to Henry VIII in 1532. Cromwell led the English Reformation for Henry but was beheaded in 1540 after falling out of the king's favor.

Francis Drake: Born in 1540, Drake was a vice admiral in the English navy and an explorer, privateer, and politician. Drake was the second person to circumnavigate the globe and was second in command when the English navy defeated the Spanish Armada in 1588.

Edward VI: As the son of Henry VIII, Edward Tudor was named king of England at age ten in 1547. He was a deeply religious king who introduced the Book of Common Prayer to the Church of England. Edward was sick his entire life and died in 1553 at age sixteen.

Elizabeth I: The Elizabethan era was named for Elizabeth Tudor, daughter of Henry VIII and Anne Boleyn, who ascended the throne at age twenty-five and served as England's queen from 1558 to 1603.

During her nearly forty-five-year reign, Elizabeth strengthened the role of the Church of England and oversaw exceptional developments in the economy, science, the arts, and military power.

Martin Frobisher: Born in Yorkshire in 1535, Frobisher was a leading Elizabethan explorer who worked as a privateer between 1555 and 1575. In the late 1570s Frobisher conducted several trips to Canada, where he searched unsuccessfully for gold. Frobisher returned to privateering in 1585 and helped defeat the Spanish Armada in 1588.

George Gower: In 1581 Elizabeth appointed Gower to the position of the official royal artist, called the serjeant painter. In 1588 Gower painted the *Armada Portrait*, one of the most famous paintings of Elizabeth.

John Hawkins: Hawkins was the first Englishman to engage in the African slave trade. He was also a successful privateer, raiding treasure ships on the Spanish Main. Hawkins was appointed treasurer of the Royal Navy in 1578 and instituted revolutionary changes in shipbuilding and design.

Henry VIII: Henry Tudor was born in 1491 and ruled England from 1509 until his death in 1547. Despite being a devout Catholic, the king dissolved all the monasteries in Britain and established the Protestant Church of England. Henry is remembered for marrying six women and beheading three of them. He was the father of three British rulers, Edward VI, Mary I, and Elizabeth I.

Nicholas Hilliard: Renaissance painter and miniaturist Hilliard was the son of an Exeter goldsmith and a student of German painter Hans Holbein the Younger. Hilliard was appointed court miniaturist and goldsmith by Elizabeth around 1570 and soon after created one of the most renowned paintings of the queen, known as *The Pelican Portrait*.

Hans Holbein the Younger: Holbein was born in Augsburg, Germany, in 1497 and was a leading printer and graphic artist. Holbein moved to England in 1536, where he painted some of the most famous portraits of Henry VIII.

Ben Jonson: Although known for his big ego and short temper, Jonson was one of the renowned playwrights of the English Renaissance. His "humours" skewered royals, aristocrats, and other playwrights, and Jonson was arrested several times for his controversial works.

Christopher Marlowe: The playwright Marlowe made a major impression on Elizabethan Renaissance theater with his histories and tragedies. Marlowe was very successful and is credited for his strong influence on Shakespeare.

Mary I: Born in 1516 to Henry VIII and Catherine of Aragon, Mary Tudor moved to reestablish Catholicism in England during her reign. Mary I earned the nickname "Bloody Mary" after ordering three hundred Protestant leaders burned at the stake.

Philip II: As the king of Spain between 1556 and his death in 1598, Philip was the leading Catholic force opposing the English Reformation. In 1588 he sent the Spanish Armada on an unsuccessful mission to conquer England and depose Elizabeth.

Walter Raleigh: Raleigh was an aristocrat, poet, and explorer, best remembered for introducing tobacco to England. Raleigh funded his own expeditions to the New World and founded the first English settlement on Roanoke Island in 1585.

William Shakespeare: Born in 1564 in Stratford-upon-Avon, Shakespeare is considered by many to be the finest playwright in the English language. Shakespeare is credited with writing more than thirty-eight plays, including the immortal *Romeo and Juliet, Macbeth*, and *A Midsummer Night's Dream*.

For Further Research

Books

Robert C. Evans, *Culture and Society in Shakespeare's Day*. New York: Chelsea House, 2012.

Brett Foster, *Shakespeare's Life*. New York: Chelsea House, 2012.

Meg Harper, *Elizabeth I: The Story of the Last Tudor Queen*. London: A&C Black, 2011.

J.E. Luebering, ed., *English Literature from the Old English Period Through the Renaissance*. New York: Rosen, 2010.

Alison Prince, *Henry VIII's Wives*. New York: Scholastic, 2011.

Mark Sengele, *Inside the Reformation*. St. Louis, MO: Concordia, 2012.

William Shakespeare, *A Midsummer-Night's Dream*. Illustrated by Arthur Rackham. London: Pook, 2012.

Websites

Elizabethan England Life (www.elizabethanenglandlife.com). This comprehensive site contains information about food, clothing, medicine, weapons, games, marriage, occupations, religion, superstitions, and dozens of other subjects concerning the daily lives of Elizabethans.

Elizabethan Era (www.elizabethan-era.org.uk). This website features extensive historical information about English life, politics, religion, and the monarchy. Visitors can discover fascinating facts about Elizabethan food, theater, sports, jobs, customs, crime and punishment, and clothing and learn about the age of exploration, the Spanish Armada, and Elizabeth I.

Elizabeth Files (www.elizabethfiles.com). This site is dedicated to all things Elizabeth I and features a gallery of paintings and images, book reviews, quotes, historic information, and important dates in the queen's life.

Middle Ages (www.middle-ages.org.uk). This site paints a vivid picture of pre-Elizabethan England between the years 1066 and 1485, with sections about royalty, religion, knights, weapons, castles, rural life, history, and the lives of women.

A Survey of London by John Stow, British History Online (www .british-history.ac.uk/source.aspx?pubid=593). John Stow wrote this account of London in 1598, near the end of Elizabeth I's reign. Stow describes the city's architecture, neighborhoods, customs, and other aspects of the Elizabethan era.

Tudor History (http://tudorhistory.org). This website is dedicated to the rulers of the Tudor dynasty, including Henry VII, Henry VIII, Mary I, and Elizabeth I. In addition to royal biographies, visitors can learn about other important people of the era and view primary texts and documents, maps, and images.

Index

Picture Credits

Cover: Thinkstock Images/Photos.com

Maury Aaseng: 21, 65

© Lebrecht Music & Arts/Corbis: 79

© National Geographic Society/Corbis: 60, 68

© The Print Collector/Corbis: 16

©Stapleton Collection/Corbis: 12

Thinkstock: 8, 9, 26, 52, 74

At the Crowning of Queen Elizabeth I, c.1940s (colour litho), Silas, Ellis (1885-1972)/Private Collection/The Bridgeman Art Library: 30

Elizabethan Townscape (gouache on paper), Doughty, C.L. (1913-85)/Private Collection/© Look and Learn/The Bridgeman Art Library: 36

Elizabeth I, Armada Portrait, c.1588 (oil on panel), Gower, George (1540-96) (attr. to)/Woburn Abbey, Bedfordshire, UK/The Bridgeman Art Library: 44

The Globe Theatre (pen & ink and w/c on paper), Cox, Paul (b.1957)/Private Collection/Photo © Chris Beetles Ltd, London/The Bridgeman Art Library: 49

About the Author

Stuart A. Kallen is the author of more than two hundred and fifty non-fiction books for children and young adults. He has written on topics ranging from the theory of relativity to the history of rock and roll. In addition, Kallen has written award-winning children's videos and television scripts. In his spare time he is a singer/songwriter/guitarist in San Diego.